WHAT OTHERS ARE SAYIN

Bruce Hills is known for his clear biblical preaching. He has been a blessing here in Singapore on many occasions. His new book, *Fearproof*, is thoroughly biblical, easy-to-read and very relevant. I recommend this book to you and believe it will inspire and challenge you to overcome the power of fear and live a life of courage for Jesus!

Rev. Dominic Yeo
*Senior Pastor, Trinity Christian Centre Singapore,
General Superintendent, The Assemblies of God Singapore*

Most people grapple with fear at some point in their life and whilst some may be able to cope well and deal with it, others I am sure will find a great resource in this book as it tackles some of the common fears that Christians experience. I am grateful that Bruce has invested time and energy to help others find freedom from fear.

James Condon
Commissioner of The Salvation Army, Australia Eastern territory

Bruce Hills engages the reader in a journey of overcoming and understanding fear. It is stingingly based in the world and an understanding of life. Putting these principles into your life will help you understand and reject the way of the enemy in trying to destroy lives. Reject fear and embrace life.

Dr Brendan Roach
President, Harvest Bible College, Melbourne Australia

FEARPROOF

How to Overcome the Paralysing Power of Fear

Exploring the '*do not fear*' statements of the Old Testament

by

Bruce Hills

CHI BOOKS

CHI-Books
PO Box 6462
Upper Mt Gravatt, Brisbane
QLD 4122, Australia

www.chibooks.org
publisher@chibooks.org

FEARPROOF
How to Overcome the Paralysing Power of Fear
Exploring the '*do not fear*' statements of the Old Testament

Copyright © 2015 by Bruce Hills

Print edition ISBN: 978-0-9942607-0-3
eBook edition ISBN: 978-0-9942607-1-0

Under International Copyright Law, all rights reserved. No part of this book may be reproduced, stored in a retrieval system, or transmitted in any form, including by any means electronic, mechanical, photocopying or otherwise in whole or in part without permission in writing from the publisher, except in the case of sermon preparation, reviews or articles and brief quotations embodied in critical articles. The use of occasional page copying for personal or group study is permitted and encouraged. Permission will be granted upon request.

Unless otherwise indicated, Scripture is taken from the, *Holy Bible, New International Version®, NIV®* Copyright © 1973, 1978, 1984, 2011 by International Bible Society. Used by permission of Zondervan. All rights reserved worldwide.

Printed in Australia, United Kingdom and the United States of America.

Distributed globally via a range of internet distribution outlets like: Ingram Book Group, Amazon.com and BookDepository.com. Distributed in the USA via Spring Arbor - Christian Alliance nationwide, Barnes & Nobel and others. Distributed in the UK and Europe through distribution outlets like Wesley Owen and Koorong UK. Also available through Chapters in Canada and Koorong in Australia.

Global eBook distribution available through outlets like Amazon Kindle, Apple iBooks, Barnes & Nobel Nook, KOBO, Koorong.com and Wesley Owen (UK).

Editorial assistance: Anne Hamilton

Cover design: Dave Stone

Layout: Jonathan Gould

Contents

Foreword	2
Introduction	3
One: Fear of Attack and Retaliation	15
Two: Fear that No–One Sees and No–One Cares	21
Three: Fear that a Cycle of Negative Circumstances Will Never End	29
Four: Fear of the Future	39
Five: Fear that We are Trapped by Our Circumstances	51
Six: Being Afraid of God Rather than the Reverential Awe (Fear) of God	57
Seven: Fear of Change	67
Eight: Fear We Haven't Got What It Takes to Do What God Has Called Us to Do	77
Nine: Fear that Past Failures Will Hinder Our Future Successes	85
Ten: Fear of Being Rejected Because of How We See Ourselves	95
Eleven: Fear that What God Has Promised Will Not Come to Pass	103
Twelve: Fear that We Will Go Without If We Give to God	113
Thirteen: Fear of the Invisible Forces of Darkness	123
Fourteen: Fear of Defeat in a Spiritual Battle	135
Fifteen: Fear of Being Overwhelmed by What We're Going Through	145
Sixteen: Fear of Satan's Intimidating Words	155
Seventeen: Fear that God Has Rejected or Forsaken Us	163
Eighteen: Fear that Our Message or Ministry Will Be Rejected	173
Nineteen: Fear that Our Best Days are in the Past	183
Twenty: Fear We Won't Be Able to Finish What We've Started	193
Conclusion	201

Foreword

From my long experience as a pastor, professional counselor, coach and mentor I can testify to the paralyzing and disabling effect of fear. Fear permeates all aspects and strata of society, is found in all personality types and attaches itself to all the pursuits of human beings. Learning how to cope with inevitable and wide-ranging fear is one of the most important and liberating lessons we can learn.

That is why Bruce Hills' book *Fearproof* is such a welcome addition to current Christian literature. It is a book that is solidly based in Scripture and well-balanced in its appreciation of the human and divine elements of emotion, human weakness and vulnerability and the much-needed dependence on divine guidance and empowering by the Holy Spirit along with personal responsibility. Through a sequential Old Testament study of 20 occurrences of the term *"Do not fear"*, Bruce has been able to draw us into the lives of Old Testament saints all of whom experienced fear, and through careful analysis provide principles and practices to overcome and manage the many facets of fear.

Fearproof is a great example of the value of reading and studying Scripture under the guidance of the Holy Spirit, and in a prayerful response, committing to apply God-given insights to the issues of daily life. Bruce has shown us how this can be done in the area of "fear". His analysis of each character study reinforces the timeless and contemporary life relevance and application of Scripture, and provides those in Christian ministry a methodology to explore other pressing issues in the same way.

Whether in my personal devotional life, my counseling, coaching and mentoring, or preaching, this book will be an important addition to my library and a practical resource in my ongoing work. Well done, Bruce!

Rev. Ric Benson
Former Senior Pastor, Kenmore Baptist Church, Brisbane, Australia
Church Consultant, Coach, Mentor and Counsellor

Introduction

Some years ago I heard the account of a British anthropologist who was studying an American Indian tribe in the late 1800s. The tribe was located in the north–eastern United States, not too far from the Canadian border. In his absorbing report he wrote about a unique ceremony this particular tribe held to initiate a boy of about 13 years old. The purpose of the ceremony was to create a *brave*.

Up to this point in the boy's life, he had been taught many skills for subsistence living: fishing, hunting and fire–making. To prove his bravery however, he had to undergo something he had not been prepared for. All the braves would take the boy deep into the surrounding forest, moving on until they came to unfamiliar territory. The boy would be escorted far from home, beyond any recognizable landmark.

When they reached the designated site, it would be nearly sunset. All the men would then leave without even the hint of a good–bye or any instructions. To prove his courage, the boy had to remain in the forest alone all night and somehow find his way back to his village.

Wisely, the first thing he'd do would be to build a fire. In that part of the United States there are grizzly bears and mountain lions, along with other dangers. Sleep would escape him as he stood vigilantly by the fire. Every time he heard a twig snap or the rustle of a bush he knew to fear the sudden onrush of one of these predators. Yet, to demonstrate his manhood, he had to wait out the night despite any inward terror or tremor.

As the first rays of dawn pierced the forest canopy, the young Indian boy would begin to get a better view of his surroundings. The first thing he would notice was that he had actually been left on a track that would lead him home. But the second and more important discovery was that somebody else was there with him. Because of the darkness, that person had been hidden from his sight. His *father* had been silently and stealthily watching over him all night with bow and arrow at the ready, protecting him against every predator.

The boy had felt vulnerable, exposed and fearful, but his fear was needless. His father had been watching over him all night.

This story is reminiscent of Psalm 121:5-8 which states:

> 'The LORD watches over you — the LORD is your shade at your right hand; the sun will not harm you by day, nor the moon by night.
>
> The LORD will keep you from all harm — he will watch over your life; the LORD will watch over your coming and going, both now and forevermore.'

Sometimes *we* feel vulnerable, exposed and fearful because of the 'dark' experiences we are enduring. No matter how dark our 'night' becomes, we do not need to fear because *our* Father is watching over us.

However, fear is a very real human emotion. How do we control, curtail or master our fears? God's Word gives us some answers.

It may come as a surprise, but the most common command God gave people in Scripture was: 'Do not fear.'[1] God knows our human nature and its propensity to fear. As we read Scripture (and we know from our own human experience), fear is often an automatic human response to unexpected tragedies, trials or overwhelming circumstances. In God's Word we read that the Lord often spoke into the lives of people in crisis, turmoil or threat with the command: 'Do not be afraid.'

The questions most inquisitive readers will be asking are, 'How do I respond to the command, "Do not fear"? How can I proactively and purposefully overcome the fears affecting *my* life?' We find the answers to these valid questions in the pages and principles of Scripture.

In this book, we will chronologically trace many of the references to '*do not fear*' in the Old Testament. This will not be an exhaustive list, but a representative list of the key times when God, or a key Old Testament character, issued the command not to be afraid. As we unpack the pages of Scripture, our quest is to identify *why* God said, 'Fear not.' In other words,

---

[1] Or equivalents such as 'fear not', 'do not be afraid' or a variation in a particular rendering or paraphrase of Scripture.

what did God reveal about himself or his purposes that became the basis for why they were instructed not to be afraid?

Each chapter looks at one Old Testament incident where the Lord said, 'Do not fear.' In each case, we'll seek to identify the specific fear which the Lord addressed, then enunciate the reasons why God told a person or group of people not to be afraid. I'm sure you'll be able to identify with the characters and circumstances and apply their lessons to the realities of your life.

Defining fear

An obvious question, then, is: 'what is fear'?

Fear has been described as many things, but here are some common definitions of fear:

- The psychological and emotional state of being afraid
- An emotion caused by impending danger, distress or dread
- Motivational speakers often use the acronym of FEAR being False Evidence Appearing Real.

Importantly, we're not seeking to address 'fear' from a psychological perspective. That is outside of my field. Our focus will be on what the Bible says about fear, and how God instructed particular people to deal with their fears.

For the sake of this book, and based on the many references in Scripture, we'll define 'fear' as 'a human emotion precipitated by being in some actual or perceived form of emotional, physical or mortal danger.'

At various times in our journey tracing the Old Testament characters, we'll see that there are degrees of fear from mild anxiety (at one end) to all out unrestrained terror (at the other).

Distinguishing a healthy fear from an unhealthy fear

There is an important distinction to clearly draw: not all fears are bad.

There is a world of difference between a good fear and a bad fear. Some fears are natural, healthy, rational and founded, whereas other fears are unnatural, unhealthy, irrational and unfounded.

Good fears protect us from imminent danger, distress and harm, whereas bad fears suffocate, distort and hamstring our lives.

Healthy fears

By way of personal example of a *healthy* fear, I openly admit that I am afraid of snakes. I live in Australia which has an abundance of venomous snakes. In fact, seven of the ten most venomous species of snakes in the world have their habitat in Australia. Some Australian species are especially dangerous, such as the Taipan, Eastern Brown, Red–belly black and Tiger—just to name a few.

I have no interest in herpetology. From the safety of my living room, I have watched documentaries and seen the late Steve Irwin confidently and cautiously pick up a 'grumpy' (to use his colloquial language for an agitated or aggressive) snake. However, I have no desire to do likewise.

The fear of snakes is not something I need exorcism from—I simply have a healthy 'fear'. I've consequently adopted the principle that, if I leave them alone, they will leave me alone. This 'fear' is not unhealthy; in fact, it protects me from potential danger.

The pre–eminent 'good' fear is what the Bible calls 'the fear of the Lord'. This 'fear' is 'God's answer to the ordinary fears that master human beings.'[2] The 'fear of the Lord' *protects* us: from sin and its consequences, from living recklessly and irresponsibly, and from anything that would tarnish our relationship with God.

It would seem, therefore, that God created us with the emotion of fear, which, in its original, pure and uncontaminated form, is designed to *protect* us from things that may hurt, harm or endanger us.

---

2 Lawrence O. Richards, Expository Dictionary of Bible Words (Grand Rapids, MI: Zondervan, 1985): 272.

Introduction

Unhealthy fears

Most people, however, struggle with *unhealthy* fears. An unhealthy fear is one that has an adverse, damaging or harmful affect upon our lives. There could be many potential sources or causes, such as:

- Consumed or riddled with anxiety
- Result of some paranormal experience like dabbling in the occult, witchcraft or an eastern religion
- Ongoing residue or consequence of trauma or tragedy
- Unresolved or untreated pain from past experiences
- Unexplainable or irrational thinking process which manifests itself in fear

As Christians seeking to grow in likeness to Christ and live a victorious life, it is imperative to identify and address any or all of the unhealthy fears at work in our lives.

To discern the difference we need to ask ourselves the following questions:

- Is this a healthy or an unhealthy fear?
- Is this a natural or an unnatural fear?
- Is this fear protecting me or is it paralysing me?
- Is this fear a positive (productive) influence in my life or is it a negative (destructive) influence in my life?

Cause of destructive and negative fear

If fear was created by God as a human emotion to protect us, how, then, did it degenerate into an emotion which can distort and damage our lives?

To answer this question, we have to go back to the first reference to fear in the Bible. When something is first mentioned in Scripture, it is often significant and revealing. The first reference to 'fear' in Scripture is linked to the tragedy of the Fall.[3] Adam and Eve were created by God as creatures of free will for the primary purpose of relationship with him. As part of their communion with

---

[3] The term 'Fall' is used in theology to describe Adam and Eve's sin and the impact on the human race.

God, they were given functions to fulfil[4] along with one command which carried severe and irreversible consequences: *'You are free to eat from any tree in the garden; but you must not eat from the tree of the knowledge of good and evil, for when you eat of it you will surely die.'* (Genesis 2:16–17)

Adam and Eve were deceived and tempted by Satan (Genesis 3:1–5). Tragically, they succumbed to temptation and ate the forbidden fruit, thus violating the one command God had given them (Genesis 3:6). They immediately became aware of their exposed state before God, both in their physical nakedness and the shame of guilt (Genesis 3:7, 10).

In a frantic but futile effort to cover themselves, Adam and Eve sewed fig leaves together to create the first form of 'clothing' (covering). The bigger question arose, though, of how they could or would 'cover' their guilt? They naïvely tried to hide from God, hoping that he couldn't see them.

This reminds me of playing 'hide and seek' with my two older children when they were very young. I finished my slow count to ten, then yelled in a ferocious tone, 'I'm coming to get you!' I heard squeals from the master bedroom, so I exaggerated my footsteps to be louder as I got nearer.

When I walked through the door, I saw them both lying face down on the bed with their heads under the pillows, but their bodies were in plain sight. They mistakenly thought that, because they couldn't see me, I couldn't see them! So, I quietly approached and grabbed both their legs while yelling, 'Gotcha!' There were two very loud screams.

The action of my kids burying their heads under the pillows is a shadow of Adam and Eve's misguided attempt to hide from God.

Genesis 3:9 records the Lord God visibly coming in the cool of the day to speak with Adam and Eve. God called out some of the saddest words in the Old Testament, *'Where are you?'*

Adam incriminated himself as he answered, *'I heard you in the garden, and I was **afraid** because I was naked; so I hid.'* (Genesis 3:9–10, emphasis mine) This is the first reference to 'fear' in the Scriptures.

---

[4] For example, take care of the garden (Genesis 2:15).

Instead of the intimate love they had been experiencing with God, Adam and Eve now feared the punishment of which they had been warned (Genesis 2:16–17). If there was a scale measuring the degree of intensity or severity of our fears, then the fear of facing God in punishment for our sin is the ultimate human fear. Death itself is the just the precursor to standing before the Living God (as eternal Judge) in accountability for our sinful lives. Many people who fear death, probably don't realise that it is actually the fear of what is beyond death (i.e. facing God) that terrifies them. Every other negative fear we experience is, to some degree, on a scale toward the ultimate fear – facing God's judgment.

As we'll see throughout this book, this is why understanding the coming of the Lord Jesus to pay the eternal price for our sin by the sacrifice of his own blood is so critical in defeating the power of fear. Through his substitutionary death he bore the punishment of our sin, through his resurrection be broke the permanence of sin, and through the indwelling of his Holy Spirit he empowers us to defeat the ongoing power of sin in our lives. By his sacrifice, we have received cleansing, forgiveness and pardon from our sins. We have access to God through Jesus Christ, eternal life beyond the grave, and an eternal inheritance that surpasses human, finite comprehension. This all means that through the redemptive work of the cross, the ultimate fear (facing God's judgment) has been defeated.

Because Jesus has defeated the ultimate fear through his death and resurrection, he can enable us, by his Spirit, to overcome every other negative fear that may be at work in our lives. In seeking to encourage Timothy to address his timidity and to exercise the gift of God in his life, Paul wrote: '...*God did not give us a spirit of timidity (fear), but a spirit of power, of love and of self-discipline.*' (2 Timothy 1:7) Paul emphasized that fear *can* be defeated. He urged Timothy not to be disempowered or contained by fear, but to overcome it by the power of the Holy Spirit.

Returning to Adam and Eve, we note that from the point when they sinned, fear degenerated from an emotion which protects people to an emotion which can also plague people. As a direct consequence of sin's corruptive and corrosive power, the protective purpose of fear was contaminated and marred.

Adam and Eve's sin not only affected them throughout their lives, but also *all* of their unborn descendants. The catastrophic consequences for all their descendants were and are unimaginable in size and scale. Because every one of us is born with an innate sinful nature, we are all born with a propensity to fear.

Unhealthy fears are some of the many consequences of the Fall. They are a perversion of God's creation caused by sin. Unhealthy fears join the ranks of other devastating invaders which sin spawned such as suffering, sickness and disease.

Faith is the antidote to fear

The Bible provides some great news. There is an antidote to fear. It is faith in God. Faith not only neutralizes but cleanses us from the toxic and acidic effect of fear.

As we progress through each chapter, we'll discover that God didn't command people to resist fear in their own strength, but to do so in faith based on a revelation of himself. In other words, God revealed something about himself that formed the basis for *why* they did not need to fear and *how* they could defeat fear.

[1] Likewise, for us, the nature of faith required in the battle against fear must be based on the revelation of God in his Word and in Christ (2 Timothy 3:16; 2 Peter 1:21; John 1:1–2, 14). Authentic and effective faith requires us to:

- Appropriate the finished work of the cross
- Trust in the Lord and lean not on one's own understanding (Proverbs 3:5)
- Be grounded in the power and promises of God (Romans 4:16–25; note vv. 20–21)
- Have received a clear 'word' from God (Hebrews 11)

Fear is an enemy of faith as the following contrasts illustrate:
- Fear reasons, worries and expects the worse, whereas *faith* believes, trusts and expects God's best

- Fear sees all that could go wrong, whereas *faith* sees a God who can do no wrong
- Fear frets at what might be, whereas *faith* anticipates what will be
- Fear feeds off vulnerabilities, whereas *faith* is fuelled by the possibilities
- Fear questions God's concern or power, whereas *faith* affirms God's unfailing concern and absolute power

To repel fear, we must allow the words of Scripture to fill and fuel our minds and hearts with faith. To endure in the battle, we also need to saturate our lives with the realities of God's Word, God's nature, God's power, God's promises, God's Spirit, God's faithfulness and God's glory.

Defeating fear requires a divine and human partnership

Subduing fear requires a vibrant partnership and cooperation between God and us. In the battle against fear, there is something only God can do and something only we can do. God's words 'do not fear' were both a command and a choice.

Divine side

In the fight against fear, what is it that only *God* can do? Strictly speaking, he's already done it. God has revealed himself as a mighty warrior in his Word. In the Old Testament, he delivered his people in mighty and miraculous ways (as we'll see). Then, in the New Testament, he reveals himself as the conquering Saviour through Jesus Christ and our ever-present help through his Holy Spirit. He helps us in the following ways:

- He sent his Son to pay the once-for-all sacrifice for our sins
- He raised his Son from the dead to break the power of sin, death and Satan
- He defeated the fear of eternal punishment beyond the grave
- He has given us his Word.
- He inhabits us through the person of the Holy Spirit.
- He will be with us on the journey (Isaiah 43:1–7, note vv. 1–5).

- He has made wonderful promises that are part of the new covenant sealed by the blood of Jesus.
- His power is unlimited and immeasurable.
- He will always be our God.

Through Christ, we are *'more than conquerors.'* (Romans 8:37) We have to trust him, depend on him and have faith in him to learn how not to fear. He will help us.

Whenever God issued the words, *do not fear*, it was a command based on a revelation of himself.

Human side

In the fight against fear, what is it that only *we* can do? On the human side, the words *'do not fear'* imply that there is a choice. The onus is on us—we must *not* fear.

One of the keys to effective Christian living is to make right choices. Our life is the sum total of the choices we have made. We must make a choice about the fears in our life.

Will we passively surrender to their power with resignation or actively address them with determination? Ultimately, this is a choice we consciously need to make. If we do not make a decision to disarm and diminish the corrosive effect of fear in our life, we have already chosen—by default—to live a life which will be defined and disempowered by fear.

Here are some of the choices we need to make:
- Choose to unmask, identify and define the fear for what it is because we can't deal with what we don't acknowledge
- Choose to recognise the damage it is doing to us
- Choose to reject it as a permanent resident in our life
- Choose that we will no longer live with that debilitating and crippling fear
- Choose to confront and face it with tenacity and determination.

We may not understand all the psychological reasons *why* the fear may have developed or *why* it is so powerful, but we do need to understand that by God's indwelling Spirit and his living Word, we can defeat its power in our lives.

Choose to adopt the renewed mindset and attitude that says, 'I want to be free! So I choose to do whatever is within my power to be free. I choose to get help in the right places to break this negative force in my life. I choose to apply the Scriptures and depend on the Spirit's transforming power to set me free.'

In the fight against fear, our responsibility is to make right choices in response to the revelation of God in his Word and in Christ.

Let's begin the journey…

1

Fear of Attack and Retaliation

Genesis 15:1

The first reference in Scripture where the words '*do not be afraid*' appear is Genesis 15:1. There it marks the start of the most profound and monumental experience in Abram's life. The phrase came at the beginning of a word from God that was part of a broader encounter that lasted from sunset one day until sunset the next.

To understand the significance and relevance of '*do not be afraid*' here, we first need to establish *why* God prefaced this whole revelation with these words.

Abram had just returned to his dwelling near the great trees of Mamre. Prior to recording Abram's experience, the author of Genesis added a transition in the narrative: '***After this****, the word of the Lord came to Abram in a vision…*' (Genesis 15:1, emphasis mine)

After what? Three things had transpired in the previous chapter which seemed to have affected Abram.

First, Abram and 318 of his trained men had just returned from successfully rescuing his nephew, Lot (Genesis 14:13–16), who had been taken captive by an alliance of Mesopotamian kings (Genesis 14:1–12, note v. 12).

Secondly, on the journey home, Abram was met by the king of Sodom—the first of two kings he would meet that day. This godless king would later offer Abram the plunders of the victory in exchange for the people of his city (who had been rescued by Abram when he went after Lot) (Genesis 14:17, 21). However Abram firmly rejected his offer.[5]

Thirdly, Abram was met by the second king—the intriguing and mysterious king of Jerusalem—Melchizedek. He was a 'priest' of God Most High who '*brought out bread and wine*', then invoked the divine blessing on Abram and received his tithe.[6]

After the success of the battle, Abram must have been feeling exposed, threatened and fearful. There is a suggestion that Abram had a disposition or tendency to fear. During a severe famine years earlier, Abram had taken Sarai to Egypt where, because of her beauty, he lied that she was his sister out of fear he would be killed (Genesis 12:12).

Now, after the victory, it appears that Abram feared possible revenge or retribution. Perhaps he was reasoning: 'I was in obscurity, but now I've burst onto the inter–tribal scene. Now I am a threat, I am vulnerable. Maybe other Mesopotamian kings like those I have just defeated will come to exert their dominance and seek retaliation.'

It is amazing how often we become very vulnerable after a success or victory.

With that background in mind, we note the rest of Genesis 15:1: '*…the word of the Lord came to Abram in a vision: "**Do not be afraid**, Abram. I am your shield, your very great reward."*'

Abram was exhorted not to fear. This was something *he* had to do. It was a choice, an action he had to initiate. Despite his inclination to fear, God required him to resolutely address the fear in his life.

---

[5] According to the custom of the day, Abram had a claim on all the recovered goods, including the people of Sodom, but he refused because he didn't want the king of Sodom to take any credit for making him wealthy. It was by God that Abram had victory, so God alone would receive the glory.

[6] Melchizedek's priesthood carries significance in the New Testament. The author of Hebrews picks up this reference in Genesis and David's use of Melchizedek in Psalm 110:4. In Hebrews 7, he deals with the relation between Melchizedek and the Lord Jesus (vv. 15–17).

Abram, however, was not instructed to resist fear by simply adopting a positive mental attitude or by exercising will power alone. Something more was needed than the power of the human mind and will—even though both of these are valid and indispensable in the fight against fear. God gave Abram *the* key to overpowering fear in his life—it was a clear 'word' of revelation of who he was as Abram's God.

> If we are to master fear and not be mastered by fear, we need a revelation of God.

In other words, to enable Abram to subdue and silence fear, God revealed things about himself. This disclosure from God of who he was and what he can and will do was all that Abram needed to neutralise and extinguish his fear. But he had to believe it by putting his faith in God.

Similarly, if we are to master fear and not be mastered by fear, we need a revelation of God. There are two primary sources of the revelation of God.

First, the Word of God (2 Timothy 3:16; cf. 1 Peter 1:21), which is the written self-revelation of God. It is the Word *of* God or *from* God, therefore a revelation *of* God and *from* God.

Secondly, the greatest revelation of God is in Jesus Christ, who is God the Son (Hebrews 1:1–3), God in flesh (John 1:14), God visible (Colossians 1:15; 2 Peter 1:16–18), and God with us (Emmanuel – Isaiah 7:14; cf. Matthew 1:23).

Being the *living* Word of God (John 1:1), Jesus is the perfect representation and fulfilment of the Scripture. Jesus is the final and greatest revelation of God. He reveals all that God is in his essence (Colossians 1:19).

The revelation of God in Christ Jesus and his Word produces faith. We have to believe in him. Faith gives us the confidence and courage to resist the power of fear.

God specifically revealed two things about himself to Abram that formed the basis for him not having to fear.

1. 'Do not fear…I am your shield…'

Abram may have felt susceptible because he had no king to watch over him, but the Lord revealed that he would be Abram's shield as *the* King over him. In essence, God said, 'Abram, you have no need to be afraid because I am watching over you as your Sovereign, and I will protect you as your Shield.' God would be a 'shield' in the sense of Protector, Defender and King.

Likewise, the Bible teaches that God is our shield (Psalm 7:10)—our sovereign and divine Protector (Psalm 91:4; Psalm 125:2). In his Word, he has promised to be, for example, our defence, fortress, refuge, rock, deliverer (Psalm 18:2), stronghold (Psalm 144:2) and hiding place (Psalm 32:7).

The Lord is over us (Psalm 91:4), around us (Psalm 125:2; 34:7), for us (Romans 8:31), with us (Hebrew 13:5b–6; cf. Deuteronomy 31:6; Psalm 118:6–7), in us (Galatians 2:20; Colossians 1:27), under us (Deuteronomy 33:27), beside us (Psalm 121:5) and behind us (Psalm 121:3).

Centuries later, King David vividly and descriptively expressed the thought of God as his protecting sovereign in the first stanza of Psalm 27:

> '*The Lord is my light and my salvation—whom shall I fear?*
>
> *The Lord is the stronghold of my life—of whom shall I be afraid?*
>
> *When evil men advance against me to devour my flesh, when my enemies and my foes attack me, they will stumble and fall.*
>
> *Though an army besiege me, my heart will not fear;*
>
> *Though war break out against me, even then will I be confident.*'
> (Psalm 27:1–3)

The Lord told Abram that he didn't need to fear because he was his shield. But then the Lord added a second dimension.

2. "Do not fear…I am…your very great reward."

This phrase is sometimes translated, '*your reward will be very great*'[7] or '*your very great reward*' in others translations. God would be both Abram's rewarder and reward. Let's briefly explore both alternatives.

One way to look at this phrase is that God promised to be Abram's *rewarder*. The context of what follows suggests that Abram interpreted this to mean that his reward would be the promised son (Genesis 15:2–3).

In a famous passage, the Lord then took him outside and asked him to count the stars before providing a promise of offspring coming from his own body as numerous as those stars (Genesis 15:4–5).

What follows is one of the most significant Scriptures in regard to Abraham and his faith: '*Abram believed the Lord, and he credited to him as righteousness.*' (cf. Romans 4:3; Galatians 3:6; James 2:23) Abram took God at his word and believed the promise.

In our lives, we can draw great encouragement from God being *our* rewarder. He provides everything we need for his purposes, plans and pleasure. He supplies everything we need to do his will. He blesses us from his lavish love. He is the giver of every good gift. As we put him first, he gives us the desires of our heart (Psalm 37:4).

Hebrews 11:6 states that God '*…rewards those who earnestly seek him.*' Ultimately, on *that* day, he will reward us for everything we have done for him.

The alternate way to look at these words is that *God* would be Abram's *reward*. If interpreted this way, God's words may be read as, 'Abram, I am all you need, all you anticipate. I am all you could ever desire. I am greater

> Despite what we gain or lose in this world and despite what we go through in this life— God is our reward.

---
7   Consistent with Genesis 12:2

than the physical blessing of land, flocks and even children. I am the fulfilment of everything you anticipate on earth. If you trust in me alone, I will be everything you need in every way at all times.'

For us, there is no greater reward in this life or the next than to know God himself. What can compare with receiving full and free forgiveness from our sins through Jesus Christ by his grace alone? What transcends having Jesus live in our lives through the indwelling of the Holy Spirit? What surpasses the hope we have of resurrection and eternal life? Despite what we gain or lose in this world and despite what we go through in this life—God is our reward.

Whether God meant that he will reward Abram or be his reward, we recognise that God is the source of both.

These two meaningful assurances were declared to Abram as the means by which he would crush fear in his life. By way of parallel, to everyone who feels threatened or intimidated by life's circumstances, on the basis of God being our Shield and Reward / Rewarder, we must make the thoughtful and intentional choice not to fear.

Many years later, God 'enabled' Abraham (as he was called then) and Sarah to conceive (Hebrews 11:11). The child of promise, Isaac, was born (Genesis 21:1–7). This sets the scene for the next chapter.

The major lesson of this opening chapter is that appropriating the revelation of God in Jesus and his Word is the way by which we confront our vulnerabilities and fears. God is our protecting King and Shield; he's everything we will ever need at all times.

2

Fear that No-One Sees and No-One Cares

Genesis 21:17–18

As a Pastor, I have heard these words more often that I can count or recall: 'no–one sees and no–one cares.' People can carry a lot of personal pain, some of which is intensely private. Unresolved and untreated pain can create a fear that we are alone and abandoned with no hope of a different future.

We're about to discover that we do not need to succumb to this fear because God hears the heartfelt cries from bruised lives.

In this chapter, we will unpack a second reference to *'do not be afraid'* in Scripture. It is found in Genesis 21:17–18. Before we examine the actual reference to *'do not be afraid'*, we need to understand the circumstances behind the story. Let's paint the background.

Background
Isaac, the son of promise, was now about three years old and had been weaned (Genesis 21:8). This meant a customary feast to celebrate his healthy growth and transition from infancy to childhood. During the festivities, Sarah noticed that Ishmael—who must have now been about fourteen or fifteen years old—was mocking (insulting and poking fun at)

Isaac (21:9). This was more than Sarah could bear, so she angrily badgered Abraham to *'get rid'* of Hagar and Ishmael so that they would have no place or claim on the future (Genesis 21:10).

This really distressed Abraham because Ishmael was his son. Nevertheless, God instructed him to listen to Sarah because there was a greater purpose invisibly unfolding. God's instruction to Abraham, however, did not mean that he didn't care about Ishmael. In fact, the Lord then reassured Abraham he would take care of Ishmael and his future lineage. This entire interaction was grounded in God's covenant relationship with Abraham (Genesis 21:12–13).

Abraham did all he could to make this heart-wrenching parting as painless and pragmatic as possible. He supplied Hagar with food and water and helped load her shoulders.

Rejected and Alone

Picture the heartache of this scene: an aged Patriarch with a heavy and despairing heart watching two lonely figures cross the horizon, knowing he will never see them again. In the distance, imagine a rejected, unsupported mother with her bewildered teenage son wandering into a barren desert and a precarious future.

Inevitably, the water ran out. Desperate for some shade Hagar helped Ishmael to lie under one of the bushes. She could not bear to see him dying slowly of dehydration and exposure. The text actually states she said to herself, '*I cannot watch the boy die.*' (Genesis 21:16) It simply broke her heart.

It would have become all the more acute as she heard his sobs. Hagar found a spot some distance away and began to weep despondently. This was a cry of helplessness, a cry of hopelessness and a cry of powerlessness.

Mixed with Hagar's cocktail of emotion was the most painful thought of all—she had done nothing wrong. She was an innocent victim.

In life, things invariably happen to us that are, like Hagar, beyond our control. It may be an unfaithful partner, a failed business, an unforeseen tragedy, a devastating diagnosis or prognosis, or even the death of someone very close.

We don't want it to happen, we don't choose for it to happen, but it does happen.

Like Hagar, we sometimes find ourselves in a desert or darkness through no fault of our own. As a consequence, we may feel we are spiritually dehydrating, despairing or directionless.

In our deepest, darkest and most desperate hour, there is a God who hears, who sees and who cares.

God *hears* our prayers

But the next verse records something wonderful: '*God **heard** the boy crying...*' (Genesis 21:17, emphasis mine)

God has revealed himself as a God who hears the cries of our heart. In our deepest, darkest and most desperate hour, there is a God who hears, who sees and who cares.

Hagar was about to discover that he was also a God who speaks and intervenes.

Let's examine the text to see what happened, remembering that our focus is on the '*do not fear*'.

> '*God heard the boy crying, and the angel of God called to Hagar from heaven and said to her, "What is the matter, Hagar? **Do not be afraid**; God has heard the boy crying as he lies there. Lift the boy up and take him by the hand, for I will make him into a great nation."*' (Genesis 21:17–18, emphasis mine)

God *sees* our needs

'*Hagar, do not be afraid,*' were the angel's words from God. Hagar's fear was blocking her memory of a previous occasion. Many years before, when she was pregnant with Ishmael, Sarai (as she was known then) had jealously expelled her. Hagar then began a long and lonely journey back to her native Egypt. She was rejected, alone and bearing Abraham's child.

As she rested from the scorching sun by the spring of Shur, the angel of the Lord appeared. Encouraging her to return, the angel assured her of the unborn child's destiny.

She didn't know this great God's name, so in Genesis 16:13 we read that '...*she gave this name to the Lord who spoke to her: "You are the God who sees me," for she said, "I have now seen the one who sees me."*'

He is the God who sees me! When she was alone in every possible way, '*the God who sees me*' intervened. By the way, there is a God who sees you in your need today.

She *felt* alone, but she wasn't actually alone. She *felt* helpless and exposed, but she wasn't actually helpless and exposed at all. God had heard her and her son's cry.

Many years later, here she was again—rejected and alone. Somehow she had forgotten about the 'God who sees me'. But God hadn't forgotten her or the covenant he had made with Ishmael's father. So God came to her by means of the voice of his angel and urged her, 'Do not be afraid.'

The message from God through the angel seems to be: 'Hagar, remember what I have done for you in the past. I am a God who hears cries from the heart. Get moving again. Lift up the boy, take him by the hand. I am going to turn everything around. This is not the end; this is a new beginning.'

> God hears our cries, God will answer our prayers and God will bring us through. He is the God who sees us. Trust him and have faith in God.

Around Easter 2012, I was preaching from this text (Genesis 21:8–21) at a large suburban church in Brisbane. At the end of the service, a lady came up to speak with me. Tears filled her eyes. Her son was serving in the Australian military and, at the time, was posted in Afghanistan where the forces were suffering a relatively high number of casualties. She shared how she had fretted for him from the day of his deployment.

But when I mentioned in the sermon about the promises God had given to Hagar, she suddenly remembered all the promises God had given her when her son was born. As she recalled those promises, her anxiety dissolved and was replaced by the peace of God. She had forgotten what God had said many years before, but when she remembered and recalled God's promises, her fear was dispelled. By this stage, she was crying and I had tears in my eyes too.

Let's remember what God has done or has said in the past.

Have faith in God

If we're crying secret tears and carrying personal pain; if we feel that no one sees and no one cares; if we're in a desert place through no fault of our own; if we feel dehydrated by loneliness and despair; or if we are incapacitated and atrophied by what we're going through, the Lord would shout a very loving and reassuring, 'Do not be afraid!'

God *hears* our cries, God will *answer* our prayers and God will bring us through. He is the God who sees us. Trust him and have faith in God.

Fear says, 'You're about to break down', but faith says, 'No, I'm about to break *through.*'

Fear says, 'All hope is gone,' but faith says, 'No, new hope is born.'

> When we respond to God in faith, we will see answers, solutions, hope, a way forward and a way through.

Fear says, 'Despair is part of my life', but faith says, 'No, despair is departing from my life.'

Fear says, 'I can see no way out', but faith says, 'I believe God will make a way out'.

God *answers* our prayers

The context implies that Hagar resisted fear and picked up her son. '*Then God opened her eyes and she saw a well of water.*' (Genesis 21:19)

Fear blinds us, but when we trust God—despite our fear—our eyes are open. When the scales of fear fell from her eyes, Hagar saw water! This was life–infusing hope. When we respond to God in faith, we, too, will see answers, solutions, hope, a way forward and a way through.

The outcome of this story was that: '*God was with the boy as he grew up. He lived in the desert and became an archer. While he was living in the Desert of Paran, his mother got a wife for him from Egypt.*' (Genesis 21:20–21)

In tying this chapter off, we note that Hagar's fear was that no–one saw and no–one cared about her and her son's predicament.

Hagar, however, was commanded not to fear for two reasons. First, because God had heard the boy's cry. Secondly, because God had given a promise to Ishmael's father, Abraham, that Ishmael would be the progenitor of a great nation (Genesis 21:13).

Lessons

How does this apply to our lives? First, whenever we feel that no–one sees and no–one cares, we need to remind ourselves that God has revealed himself as (to use Hagar's words) 'the God who sees me'.

He sees, he knows and he cares.

If we are experiencing desolation or desperation, we do not need to fear because he is a God who hears the cries of our heart. He can open *our* eyes so that we can *see* a way forward and a way through the circumstance.

Secondly, God promised Abraham that he would take care of the boy because of the covenant he made to bless his offspring (Genesis 12:1–3; 15:1–21; 17:1–22). God was faithful to his covenant by responding to Ishmael's sobs. Through the angel, the Lord reassured Hagar that he would make him into a 'great nation'.

By way of parallel, when we feel abandoned and vulnerable because of the circumstances in which we find ourselves, we must remember that God is a covenant–making and covenant–keeping God. Through Christ Jesus he has initiated a new covenant that has been sealed by Jesus' blood. This covenant brings many promises that we need to regularly remember.

He promises:

- answers to prayer (Psalm 91:14–16)
- his continual presence (Matthew 28:20; Hebrews 13:5)
- inward strength from his indwelling Spirit's power (Ephesians 3:16)
- the hope of an eternal future (Titus 2:13; 1 Peter 1:3–4)

Therefore do not fear! We're never alone. He is the God who sees us, hears our cries and will answer our prayers.

3

Fear that a Cycle of Negative Circumstances Will Never End

Genesis 26:23–24

When I was a young boy living in Brisbane in the early 1970s, I vividly remember being taken by a couple of older girls from our church to the 'Exhibition', locally known as the 'Ekka'. It was the annual showcase of farming, livestock, agriculture and general community wares.

Aside from the displays, there were also carnival–style fun rides. One of these was the 'Octopus'—it had eight 'legs' with small open–top 'cages' seating up to four people. The 'Octopus' would spin clockwise while each individual cage would independently spin anti–clockwise. We decided to all go on it.

The reason this day is etched in my memory is that I experienced fear on a hitherto unprecedented scale. This ride kept going faster and faster. The g–forces threatened to propel me out of the cage (or that's how it felt). I started to call out to the operator to stop, but I am convinced he sadistically just made it go even faster.

The young ladies looking after me tried to console and comfort me but I was riddled with terror. The ride felt interminable and the sheer panic unending. Finally the torment and torture finished, but I was so traumatised that, even to this day, I rarely go on rides.

Like that ordeal on the 'Octopus', we sometimes experience seasons in life where it seems everything is going wrong. A cluster of events brings us to the point where we say, 'I don't know if I can take any more!'

If it were one thing in isolation, we'd probably be ok, but hit after hit can drain even the most resilient people. I have been in that position a couple of times in my life.

Even as I write this chapter, I am *just* on the other side of the most difficult series of circumstances I have ever endured. Negative spirals can produce a fear that manifests itself in the words, 'Will this cycle ever end?'

Good news! God is faithful. The cycle will end. God will bring us through. He knows our limits. The fear that the terrifying 'ride' will never stop does not need to incapacitate us any longer.

We find this scenario illustrated in our third reference to '*do not fear*' in the Old Testament which is found in Genesis 26:23–24.

The prevailing circumstance was a devastating famine in the land. Isaac had to make a critical decision: Would he go down to Egypt—as his father, Abraham, had done in a previous famine—or stay in Gerar on the fertile coastal plains? God gave him clear instructions: '*Do not go down to Egypt; live in the land where I tell you to live. Stay in this land for a while…*' (Genesis 26:2)

At times we need to 'move on' from negative experiences before we can flourish.

Then God renewed to Isaac the promise he first made to Abraham his father. Through Isaac, God was going to continue fulfilling his promise to Abraham. So Isaac stayed where he was in Gerar (Genesis 26:3–6).

Isaac's cycle of trouble

After this extraordinary promise from God, two events occurred that had a bearing on this reference to *'do not fear'*.

First, Isaac got into trouble by lying (Genesis 26:7–11). He told Abimelech that his gorgeous wife, Rebekah, was his sister. One day, however, Abimelech saw Isaac 'caressing' Rebekah which exposed his lie and caused some awkward moments.

Secondly, Isaac experienced a lot of friction (Genesis 26:12–22). Despite the famine, Isaac flourished because the Lord was blessing him. Unsurprisingly, the Philistines—with whom he co-existed—became jealous of his prosperity and ordered him to move away. Isaac moved to the Valley of Gerar where he unstopped the wells opened during his father's time.

This, too, brought contention because the local herdsmen claimed these newly opened wells as their own. Twice this happened. These two wells became unwelcome causes of disagreement in this season of his life. Isaac named those two wells *Esek* which means 'dispute' and *Sitnah* which means 'opposition'.

Verse 22 records that Isaac *'…moved on from there and dug another well, and no one quarrelled over it.'* He moved *on* from the place of resistance and disagreement to a new place where his men dug a new well. This time no one quarrelled over it. Isaac had to *move on* from yesterday's contentious experiences before he found a new place where he would flourish.

He named the new well *Rehoboth* which means 'room' or 'broad places'. At times we, too, need to 'move on' from negative experiences before we can flourish.

Before we examine the reference to *'do not be afraid'*, let's do a quick recap. Isaac was in the middle of a crippling and severe famine; he nearly got killed for lying to his hosts about his wife; because he prospered, the neighbours were provoked and asked him to leave the region; and every time he dug a well to water his flocks, the local herdsmen disputed with him.

Do not be afraid

It seemed everywhere he went there was trouble and turmoil. Then we read that from Rehoboth, Isaac '...*went up to Beersheba. That night the Lord appeared to him and said, "I am the God of your father Abraham.* **Do not be afraid***, for I am with you; I will bless you and will increase the number of your descendants for the sake of my servant Abraham."*' (Genesis 26:23–24, emphasis mine)

> God Almighty is with us in any and every circumstance actively shaping and sculpting our lives into Christ's image.

Finally, he arrived at a place (Beersheba) where there was peace. But there was a hint here that the sum total of the famine, threats, disputes and contentions had taken an emotional toll. Could Isaac have been reasoning along the lines: 'Is life just going from one challenge to another? Is life just one hardship after another? Is this cycle ever going to end?'

I would suggest this is why the Lord had to say, 'Do not be afraid.' Put in contemporary terms, God was saying, 'Isaac, I am your God as I have been your father's God. I will give you good reasons why you shouldn't fear despite all the ups and downs of your life at the moment. Firstly, '*I am with you*.' (Genesis 26:24) You have my continual presence. I am watching over you. Everywhere you go—even through difficult circumstances—I am there *with* you to bring you through. Secondly, you have my promise and my covenant, '...*I will bless you and will increase the number of your descendants for the sake of my servant Abraham.*' (Genesis 26:24) Therefore, I am not going to let you down. You will come through. I will accomplish what I have said. I will do what I have promised. I will be faithful to the covenant. You have my presence, my promise and my covenant. So '*do not be afraid.*'

Application
May we draw strength from God's assurance to Isaac in Genesis 26:23–24 because there are many parallels with our lives. We, too, are in covenant with God through the blood of Jesus Christ, a covenant that possesses great promises. The Holy Spirit is living within us as God's guiding and empowering presence. God Almighty is with us in any and every circumstance actively shaping and sculpting our lives into Christ's image.

Sometimes we, too, have seasons of ups and downs that may make life feel like a roller–coaster. Maybe we're even questioning whether the rest of our life is going to be an endless repetition of up and down, round and round.

Very subtly and insidiously, fear creeps in and persuasively argues that things won't change. The encouragement from this story is that we do not need to fear. God promises his presence to finish what he has started in our life. His divine presence will bring us through anything and everything strongly and maturely.

Lessons from Isaac
Before concluding this chapter, we should note Isaac's *response* to the promise and revelation of God: '*Isaac built an altar there and called on the name of the Lord. There he pitched his tent, and there his servants dug a well.*' (Genesis 26:25)

There are four applications we can draw from Isaac's response in verse 25. Whenever we are in a cycle of trying circumstances, here are some biblical principles for how we can move forward.

1. Isaac 'built an altar'
An 'altar' in the Old Testament generally is a 'type' or 'symbol' of worship.[8] An altar was a place of meeting with God through sacrifice.

---

[8] Other references to altars being constructed are: Noah (Genesis 8:20), Abraham (Genesis 12:7; 13:4; 22:9), Jacob (Genesis 33:20) and Moses (Exodus 17:15; 20:24–26). In the Tabernacle and later in the Temple, there were two altars: one for burnt offerings (Exodus 27:8; cf. 2 Chronicles 4:1) and the other for incense (Exodus 39:38; cf. 1 Kings 6:20; 1 Chronicles 28:18).

The fulfilment of these Old Testament 'shadows' (Hebrews 8:5; 10:1) was Christ's sacrificial (Hebrews 9:14) and intercessory ministry (John 17:1–16; Hebrews 7:25). Now we, as believer–priests, offer the spiritual sacrifices of praise and worship (Hebrews 13:15). The lessons here are:

- Foster and maintain a heart of worship
- Keep communing with God in intimacy through Christ Jesus
- Keep our lives (heart and mind) clean.

> Worship keeps us anchored to the unchanging and unshakable realities of God.

It is imperative that in the difficult seasons of life we keep engaging with God through worship. He has not changed (and does not change), but we do and our experiences do.

Worship keeps us anchored to the unchanging and unshakable realities of God.

2. Isaac 'called on the name of the Lord'

The 'name' of God represents his character and nature. Calling on the 'name of the Lord' speaks of seeking God. There are many aspects of seeking God, such as:

- Crying out to God in time of need (2 Samuel 22:7; cf. Psalm 18:6)
- Praying for divine intervention (Psalm 99:6; 1 Kings 18:24; 2 Chronicles 20:4)
- Devoting time to wait upon God for answers or guidance (2 Chronicles 11:16; 26:5; Daniel 9:3; Hosea 10:12)
- Intentionally pursuing God and his face (Genesis 4:26; 12:8; 1 Chronicles 16:8; Isaiah 55:6)
- Putting God and his ways as our highest priority (2 Chronicles 17:4; 26:5; Ezra 8:21; Matthew 6:33)

Like Isaac, we need to persevere in seeking for more of God in the challenging times of life. We have an assurance that if we seek him with all our hearts, we *will* find him (Jeremiah 29:13–14; Deuteronomy 4:29).

Persist in the practice of prayer. Pray boldly, specifically and with a heart of thanks.

3. Isaac 'pitched his tent'

As we have seen, because of the famine and inter-tribal tensions, Isaac had been moving from place to place. We also noted, that until he arrived at Beersheba, there are suggestions he was agitated and fearful.

But after God's clear word to him to *not fear*, it was time to settle down.

'Pitching a tent' spoke of establishing himself. Rather than living a transitory life, it was now time to put down his roots. Pitching a tent is also indicative that Isaac was claiming land for himself and his family.

When people are fearful or in turbulent times, they often feel that the answer would be a change of church, home, location or job. The remedy, however, is not an external change of environment, but an internal change of attitude. Or, in different words, not a shift in our location, but a shift in our mindset by pitching *our* tent.

Pitching our tent has a number of applications in contemporary life such as:

- Planting ourselves in a local church. Be involved. Serve. Honour the pastor. Pray for the church. Exercise your gift. Give generously. Love the house of God. Change in the church starts with church in us!
- Stay where we are living until God gives very clear guidance to do otherwise. I once heard expatriate Aussie speaker, Mal Fletcher, say, 'Never move out of *frustration*; move out of *revelation*.' Don't pursue a tree-change or a sea-change until we have first sought personal-change.
- Work hard in our current place of employment or study. Conscientiously seek to do our best as if we were working for Jesus

as our employer (Colossians 3:23–24; Ephesians 6:7). Work industriously, ethically, creatively and respectfully (Titus 2:9–10; Ephesians 6:5–9). If we're consistently unhappy in our workplace then we either need to change our attitude or prayerfully look for a new job.

> God promises his presence to finish and fulfil what he has started.

4. Isaac's servants 'dug a well'

Water is a basic necessity of life. Rain rarely fell around Beersheba or the region where Isaac was living, but the geological structure provided the region with many springs (Deuteronomy 8:7).

Isaac's servants sank a shaft or bored a hole to access the natural underground springs. The water from the well would supply their need for hydration, cooking and watering their flocks. The process of digging a well was part of the way Isaac would sustain his family, servants and herds.

The lesson for us is to dig our own well. In non–metaphorical language, this can mean to:

- Dig into the Scriptures everyday so we keep our spiritual life hydrated by the life–giving Word of God (1 Peter 2:2; Psalm 1:1–3, note v. 3)
- Keep full of the Holy Spirit so the 'rivers of living water' can flow from within us (John 7:37–39)
- Keep seeking and pursuing God for more of him (Isaiah 55, note vv. 1, 6 & 10)
- Maintain a freshness in our daily relationship with Jesus so that our experience never grows cold or stale

Chapter Three

Lessons

The central theme of this chapter is that, if we feel that life has been one crisis after another, we do not need to fear because God promises his presence to finish and fulfil what he has started. Like Isaac, we need to *respond* in faith by maintaining a heart of worship, seeking God, establishing ourselves and 'digging' into the things of God in fresh ways.

4

Fear of the Future

Genesis 46:3–4

Australia is a nation of migrants. Over two hundred years ago, early voluntary (and many involuntary) migrants from Great Britain forged a new nation. Could they ever have foreseen how Australia would develop? Naturally, they could not, but they all contributed to Australia's collective history which has made the nation what it is today.

The ramifications of our choices

We must understand that our decisions about the future have a bearing far beyond our own lives. Therefore, we have a responsibility to keep moving, growing, developing, changing, serving, praying, witnessing, believing, encouraging and experiencing God.

This is not just for our sakes, but also for the sakes of those who follow us. Our lives are influencing people one way or the other. Our lives are shaping the future one way or the other.

Sadly, some people stop growing at crucial points. They fail to realise the ramifications not just for their own lives but for those whom they influence. Often the principal cause of not moving forward is an incapacitating fear of the future.

Every now and then we are faced with a critical choice: to embrace the future with hope or stay 'parked'. In this chapter, we will explore one man's journey facing the future and the fear which nearly restrained him.

Historical setting

As a fourth reference to '*do not fear*', we will focus on the Patriarch Jacob. Our examination of Jacob's story spans from Genesis 45:25 – 46:4, but we'll particularly focus on just two verses found in 46:3-4.

Let's set the scene. The entire region (which we would now call the Middle East) was in the stranglehold of another severe famine. This food shortage had been foretold by Joseph as the interpretation of Pharaoh's dreams. Our study Scripture (Gen. 45:25–46:4) lies in the second year of the seven year period of famine.

Joseph, now Prime Minister of Egypt, had revealed to his eleven brothers who he was. Joseph provided them with supplies, provisions and carts for them to go back and bring their father, Jacob, and their families to live in Egypt.

There are a number of principles in Jacob's story which help us to understand why we shouldn't fear the future.

The future is full of hope

After the eleven brothers arrived back in Canaan they told Jacob, '*Joseph is still alive! In fact, he is ruler in Egypt.*' (Genesis 45:26) Jacob was initially stunned by disbelief. Emotionally seized by the shock he could barely absorb their words. Could he dare believe this news and raise his shipwrecked hope?

For twenty–two years, Jacob had been grieving since he was deceptively told that his favourite son, Joseph, had been torn to pieces by a wild animal. The deceiver himself had been deceived. He had been inconsolable. Something within him had died (Genesis 37:35).

All these years later he was told, '*Joseph is still alive!*' He simply couldn't believe it (see v. 26). '*But when they told him everything Joseph had said to* them, *and when he saw the carts Joseph had sent to carry him back, **the spirit of their father Jacob revived.**'* (v. 27, emphasis mine)

Like Jacob, tragedy, trauma, pain, shock, conflict or contradiction can cause some of us to inwardly shut down. Our spirit withers. Our expectation *of* and *for* the future shrivels. Our lives become mechanical and mundane, distant and detached.

But when Jacob heard that the future had hope, his spirit *revived*. In the same way, despite the horror of what we may have endured in our lives, God wants us to realize the future is full of hope.

> If we will believe and trust God, his grace and power can reach into the inner recesses of our souls and bring life to the deadness.

If we will believe and trust God, his grace and power can reach into the inner recesses of our souls and bring life to the deadness.

There is no darkness within us that the light of his presence and power cannot illuminate and irradiate. There is no experience or pain that he does not identify or sympathise with, so therefore he is able to strengthen and enable us to come through anything and everything (Ephesians 3:16; Hebrews 4:15–16). There is no place from which he cannot lead us out onto the pathway to wholeness (Psalm 23:2).

Just as the '*…spirit of their father Jacob revived*', so God can revive *our* spirits with excitement and expectation for the future.

With his spirit revived, Jacob said, '*I'm convinced! My son Joseph is still alive. I will go and see him before I die.*' (v. 28)

What a contrast in his vocabulary from '*…in mourning will I go down to the grave to my son*' (Genesis 37:35) to '*…I will go and see him **before** I die*'

(Genesis 45:28, emphasis mine). Hope transforms our spiritual vocabulary of desolation to the language of expectation, from a vocabulary of death to a language of life, from a vocabulary of hopelessness to the language of faith.

We do not need to fear the future because the future is full of hope. When the reality of that hope fills our hearts, our spirits are revived. This inevitably transforms our outlook. A change of outlook changes the way we speak.

God is with us on the journey (into the future)

A second reason why we should not fear the future is because God is with us on the journey. Jacob had begun the journey. He had uprooted himself from the life and land he had known to travel to the unknown. God was with him on the journey.

The first stop was 'Beersheba' which was a significant place in his and his family's collective history.[9] A number of noteworthy things had transpired here:

- Esau had sold his birthright to Jacob (Genesis 25:29–34)
- Jacob deceived Isaac into giving the blessing of the first born which should have been reserved for Esau (Genesis 27:1–29)
- Esau consequently determined to kill Jacob because of what he had done (Genesis 27:41)
- Rebekah, Jacob's mother, then instructed Jacob to escape from Esau's murderous intent by fleeing to his uncle Laban in Paddam Aram

Beersheba was a place of very mixed, maybe raw, emotions. The last time he ventured beyond Beersheba, it had been a turbulent journey. On the positive side, this journey had resulted in:

- Receiving a God–given dream at Bethel (Genesis 28:10–22)

---

[9] 'Beersheba' means 'well of oath' or 'well of seven'. It got its name from being the place where Abraham made an oath with Abimelech senior. Abraham had given Abimelech seven lambs to validate and substantiate that he had genuinely and personally dug the well they disputed over. It then became a favourite residence for Abraham and Isaac.

- Falling in love with Rachel (Genesis 29:18) and obtaining another wife, Leah (Genesis 29:23–25), along with their respective maids, Bilhah (Genesis 30:4–5) and Zilpah (Genesis 30:9–10)
- Producing twelve sons; and prospering in an amazing way (Genesis 30:43)

On the negative side, however, Jacob:
- was exploited by Laban
- was deceived into receiving Leah as his wife rather than Rachel
- Worked an additional seven years for Rachel
- Expected to confront Esau which was probably the most daunting of all

Aside from the long history of Beersheba to Jacob and his family, it was also the last outpost in the Promised Land. Beersheba was the frontier into the unknown. After Beersheba, it was uncharted and unfamiliar territory for Jacob.

Added to this was the memory that his grandfather, Abraham, got into a lot of trouble when he went to Egypt. In fact, Abraham had been expelled (Genesis 12:20). His father, Isaac, had been expressly forbidden to go to Egypt even though there was a virulent famine in his homeland (Genesis 26:2). Here was Jacob, back in Beersheba, and about to sojourn into Egypt, a place he'd never been before.

At Beersheba, however, Jacob responded positively: '...*he offered sacrifices to the God of his father Isaac.*' (Genesis 46:1) In essence, this means that Jacob sought God, he reached out to God, he prayed—he got serious about hearing from God.

There is a hint in this verse (Genesis 46:1) that maybe the return to Beersheba unsettled Jacob. Forensically, we work back from God's reply in verses 3–4 (which we will observe in the next point) to see what he may have been thinking.

It seems Jacob was seeking reassurance: 'Am I on the right track? Is this the best thing for my family's future? Will I remain in God's will? Will God be

> We do not need to fear the future because God is with us on the journey.

with me? God, I need to hear from you. Lord, the last time I was facing an uncertain future you appeared to me in a dream at Bethel and assured me of my future. Lord, I need your word afresh and anew.'

We may possibly be at a 'Beersheba' in our life at the moment. Maybe we're uncertain or unsettled about the direction of our life at the moment. Or perhaps some memories and wounds make us reticent or hesitant to make certain decisions about the future. We may possibly be on the frontier of a new dimension in God and we're about to step into the unknown, but what lies ahead is daunting because it is beyond the range of our experience.

What should we do?

We should do what Jacob did and get serious about touching God by engaging in a time of sacrificial prayer. This means praying with perseverance, determination and passion. Dedicate time to pursue God. Let's discipline and position ourselves to hear from God. It is worth investing time to seek God about the future, otherwise we may be unintentionally allowing fear to chain us to the past.

As the people of God, we don't want to live our lives randomly or without any sense of God or the knowledge of his will. We need to hear from God, live in his presence, genuinely know his will and integrate our lives around his purposes.

The best thing we can do to get some clarity, reassurance and guidance is to call upon his name with all our heart.

We do not need to fear the future because God is with us on the journey. He welcomes us to call upon his name, seek his face and listen for his voice.

God's promises about the future will be fulfilled

Jacob made his sacrifices and duly went to bed. While he slept, God spoke to him in a vision (Genesis 46:2). The clear lesson here is that if we call, he will answer.

Let's examine God's specific words to Jacob in the vision: '"I am God, the God of your father," he said. "Do not be afraid to go down to Egypt, for I will make you into a great nation there. I will go down with you, and I will surely bring you back again. And Joseph's own hand will close your eyes."' (Genesis 46:3–4)

The Lord revealed himself as the God of Jacob's past ('*I am…the God of your father…*') and Jacob's future ('*Do not be afraid to go down to Egypt…*'). The Lord revealed himself as a God of purposes and plans, a God of personal care, and a God of restoration.

> Our lives in Christ are like the intricate pieces of a living jigsaw puzzle—it is only as pieces fit together that we start to see the whole picture.

Essentially, God gave four promises to Jacob for *why* he did not need to fear going to Egypt. Each one has applicability to our future.

1. '…for I will make you into a great nation *there*.'

God revealed to Jacob that the future expansion of his family would take place '*there*' (Egypt). Jacob was not to be afraid of going to Egypt because it would be the place where God would fulfil his future purposes for his life and posterity.

God is sovereign, which, in short, means that God can do what he wills, how he wills, when he wills and *where* he wills. It may not have made sense to Jacob that God's future purposes would be accomplished in Egypt. It didn't have to make sense to Jacob. It wasn't *his* plan, but God's.

> We do not need to fear the twists and turns of life because we know that we are not alone—the Lord is with us.

Equally, there may be times when God will lead us to the equivalent of Jacob's 'Egypt'. It may not make sense to us ('why Egypt'?), but it doesn't have to make sense to us. It is not *our* plan or purpose; it is God's. We are all part of a big picture, a great purpose and a vast plan.

Our lives in Christ are like the intricate pieces of a living jigsaw puzzle—it is only as pieces fit together that we start to see the whole picture. We are like the different coloured threads of a tapestry—it is only as the weaver knits them together with other threads that the design is seen. Or, to employ another metaphor, we are like an instrument in an orchestra—it is only as we play our part in harmony with the other instruments that the symphony is fully heard.

We don't have to understand the big picture; we just have to understand what we have to do and do it—even if it means going where we have never been before—even if it means doing what we have never done before—even if it means becoming what we have never been before.

'Jacob (you could inset your name), do not be afraid to go into the uncharted, because I am going to fulfil my purposes for you *there*.'

2. 'I will go down to Egypt *with* you…'

A second reason we can deduce as to why Jacob was told not to fear was the assurance of God's abiding and accompanying presence. In different words, it was as if God reassured him, 'I will be with you on the journey. You will never be alone.'

Likewise, in our journey of faith, in the pilgrimage of our lives toward God's heart and purpose, we must consciously remember that God is with us. We do not need to fear the twists and turns of life because we know that we are not alone—the Lord is with us. This is suggestive of God's words to Joshua: '*The Lord himself goes before you and will be with you; he will never leave you nor forsake you. Do not be afraid; do not be discouraged.*' (Deuteronomy 31:8)

3. '…and I will surely bring you back again.'
Realistically, this particular promise would come to pass beyond Jacob's lifetime. Jacob, however, was encouraged not to fear because God's purposes are generational.

We could rephrase this promise as: 'Jacob, I will bring your descendants back to this land of promise. You will not personally see it, but know that I will do something through you that will go on and on through many generations.'

Our lives are part of God's purposes to serve and influence *our* generation, but God's purposes unfold throughout many generations. He desires to do something in and through us that outlives our lifetime.

In our local churches, we should:
- Celebrate and champion those who have kept their spirit fresh and vital
- Honour those whose lives have been dedicated to God
- Value those who serve tirelessly and sacrificially
- Admire those whose faith and character have been unshakable and say a big 'thank you' for their legacy

Allow me to address those readers who would regard themselves as mature in the faith. Please keep moving into God's unfinished purposes for your lives and embrace God–initiated change.

But to those who have stopped growing and, like Jacob, may be paralysed by pain let me say this: Even if you don't grow for your own sake, grow for the sake of your family. Don't let the future generations perpetuate your pain. We have to leave a legacy for our children's children. What spiritual legacy and example of faith are you leaving for your kids (and maybe grandkids)?

If we don't grow, if we allow fear to make us inflexible or immovable, it won't just affect our lives—it will affect those around us and thwart the potential of the purpose of God.

For God to fulfil his purposes for his chosen people, Jacob had to keep moving on—despite his fear.

4. 'And Joseph's own hand will close your eyes.'

This fourth promise must have been the most moving of all for Jacob. His eleventh son, Joseph, whom he had assumed was dead, would be there at his death.

> Let's not be afraid to come to God with our pain and let him continue the process toward our wholeness.

Perhaps Jacob feared raising his hopes to believe that his long held pain would be healed. Through these words God reassured him, 'Jacob, you do not need to fear making yourself vulnerable again… do not fear hoping again… don't be afraid to move on from your painful experiences. All the years of pain will be healed in a moment. I am going to restore you. I care about the most personal details of your life. If you trust me and follow me, you will finish strongly.'

Similarly, in our lives, we are reassured today that God cares about our personal world. He is a God of healing and restoring power. Don't stop believing that the best is yet to come. Let's not be afraid to come to God with our pain and let him continue the process toward our wholeness.

Even though he had been through a difficult and painful season (lasting 22 years), the Lord in essence said, 'Do not be afraid of what is ahead. If you could know what I know you would give no place to fear at all. I will accomplish through you and your descendants what I have promised.'

Finally

After receiving this reassuring word from God, we read that Jacob, his sons, daughters, their spouses and children all went to Egypt. There he was emotionally reunited with his son, Joseph. Jacob and his family were settled in the most fertile place in Egypt (Goshen) where they thrived, prospered and became a great people.

If *our* lives are centred on God and his purposes, we do not need to fear the future because the future is full of hope, his presence will be with us wherever we go and God has made astounding promises that will be fulfilled.

5

Fear that We are Trapped by Our Circumstances

Exodus 14:13–14

My central ministry role is to train and equip pastors and leaders in strategic mission centres throughout the majority world. This takes me to nations such as Burkina Faso, Pakistan and Bangladesh.

On several occasions, I have been asked, 'What is the worst traffic you have ever experienced in your travels?' Three places immediately spring to mind in equal first place: Dhaka (Bangladesh), Nairobi (Kenya) and Cairo (Egypt).

The traffic is unbelievable. No-one takes any notice of the traffic lights, advisory signs or even the police! Three lanes may be marked but there are five lanes of traffic all crawling forward to gain some advantage. The primary way drivers indicate they are changing lanes is by using their horn. Often the car in which I am travelling is completely surrounded by suffocating traffic. It brings a feeling of utter powerlessness and paralysis— no way forward and no way back.

About 400 years after the death of Joseph, the Israelites found themselves in a much worse position than being stuck in gridlocked traffic. This is graphically described in a fifth biblical reference to '*do not fear*', which we find in Exodus 14:10–14, particularly verses 13–14.

Historical background

The nation of Egypt had been decimated by the ten plagues. The Egyptian people were grief–stricken by the death of the first born of every family. In fact, '*…there was not a house without someone dead.*' (Exodus 12:30)

Under Moses' leadership, the Israelites had been freed from Egyptian captivity and were now on their march to the Promised Land. To avoid confrontation with the Philistines who lived on or near the coastal plains, the Lord directed the Israelites through the longer desert route.

Then, as a tactic, God led them on a roundabout route to give Pharaoh the impression that they were wandering aimlessly and rudderless. God's purpose in doing this was to draw Pharaoh and his forces out so he could display his glory.

Everything went according to plan because some days later Pharaoh changed his attitude toward the Israelites. In his view, the Egyptian labour force was wandering in the desert. The Lord hardened Pharaoh's heart so he amassed a huge, mobile, highly equipped and regimented army to bring the Israelites back. They set out in pursuit of the Israelites.

> Adversity unveils what is within our heart. We really see the measure and maturity of our faith in times of crises.

It didn't take long for Pharaoh and his army to corner the Israelites. On one side, the Israelites had the impassable Red Sea. On the other, they had the threatening and menacing Egyptian army thundering toward them. There seemed to be no escape. Being utterly terrified, they cried out to God for intervention.

Their unbridled fear mutated into anger toward Moses: '*Was it because there were no graves in Egypt that you* brought us to the desert to die? What have you done by bringing us out of Egypt? Didn't we say to you in Egypt, "Leave us alone; let us serve the Egyptians"? It would have been better for us to serve the Egyptians than to die in the desert!' (Exodus 14:11–12)

Because they were filled with fear, the people could never have imagined that God was about to do something miraculous for them. With terror clouding their thoughts, the Israelites didn't know that God was going to use this very circumstance to demonstrate his glory. Little did they realise that this seeming tragedy was about to become one of their defining moments as a people.

In the present moment, though, fear smothered their faith.

In one sense, it is quite understandable why the people were in fear. They were completely surrounded with no obvious, visible way out. There were only two alternatives—certain death or a return to slavery and probable punishment.

So, sadly, the mentality of the children of Israel was one of resignation, degeneration and faithlessness. They were about to capitulate and return to captivity in Egypt.

Adversity unveils what is within our heart. We really see the measure and maturity of our faith in times of crises. Our trust in God is tested when we're faced with impossibility.

Stand Firm

Against this backdrop we then read Moses' heroic words: '...***Do not be afraid. Stand firm*** *and you will see the deliverance the Lord will bring you today. The Egyptians you see today you will never see again. The Lord will fight for you; you need only be still.*' (Exodus 14:13–14, emphasis mine).

'Standing firm' speaks of an inward disposition of resolve, determination, strength, courage, endurance and faith.

Rather than being riddled by fear, Moses told them to adopt a different posture: *Stand firm!* Naturally, this didn't mean that he wanted the people to literally stand rigid and not move a muscle. It was more to do with the posture of their hearts. 'Standing firm' speaks of an inward disposition of resolve, determination, strength, courage, endurance and faith.

Moses did not say, 'stand firm' into a vacuum as if it depended on dogged human will power. On the contrary, he told them to stand firm by focusing on what God was about to do: '***Stand firm*** *and you will see the deliverance the Lord will bring you today.*'

We, too, can 'stand firm' by focussing on what our God can do.

Why the Israelites should not fear

Moses explicitly outlined the reasons why they were not to fear, namely, '*The Egyptians you see today you will never see again. The Lord will fight for you; you need only be still.*' (Exodus 14:13–14)

First, the deliverance would be so decisive and tangible that the visible enemy—the Egyptians—whom they could see would never be seen again. This victory was going to be so comprehensive that the force that had oppressed them for years was going to be broken once and for all. They were going to be delivered from intimidation and the intimidator in one powerful act of God.

Secondly, the Lord promised that he would fight *for* them. Here is a paraphrase of Moses' words: 'People of God, this is not your battle alone. Your God is on your side. He will fight for you. He will give you strength. He will give you the victory. He will defeat and decimate the power of your past oppressor. He can give you the resolve to go on. Do what you know to do. Do what God has told you to do and he will do what he alone can do.'

In response to these two reasons why the people weren't to fear, Moses indicated they '*…need only be still.*' All they had to do was watch on as God dealt with the enemy. What does 'still' mean in this sense?

- Consciously resist the natural impulse to fear by giving no place to fear, anxiety or fretting (Exodus 14:13)

- Depend upon God's strength to bring them through
- Expect divine intervention because something beyond natural ability was needed
- Trust unreservedly in God's love and power (Psalm 20:7–8)

We can draw many applications from Moses' words to the people. If we are to master fear, we must depend solely on God in implicit trust as we stand firm.

Being 'still' does not imply inactivity. On the contrary, it is an active response. It means to exercise *active* faith and to trust in God and his promises.

Moses conveyed the heart of God by saying, in essence: 'I didn't bring you this far to desert you and leave you to the mercy of your enemies. I didn't deliver you from slavery only to allow you to return to slavery. I didn't judge your oppressors only to allow them to oppress you all over again. I promised you a land. I promised you a future. You are my people. Stop expecting the worst to happen. Watch, learn and see what kind of God I am.'

After this, God responded to Moses: '*Why are you crying out to me? Tell the Israelites to move on. Raise your staff and stretch out your hand…*' (Exodus 14:15–16a)

Phrased differently, it seemed that God was asking, 'Why are you belly-aching? Why don't you trust me? Haven't you seen my power in the past? Don't you remember what I did in Egypt? Move on. Stop wallowing and start walking.'

The outcome: The angel of God which had been in front of the Israelites moved behind them. The pillar of cloud also went behind them forming an impenetrable and visible barrier. Throughout the night there was light on the Israelite side and darkness on the Egyptian side.

At God's command, Moses stretched out his hand over the Red Sea. A strong east wind drove the sea back so that the body of water was divided.

> The impossible and impassable are no obstacles for God. God can make a way where there is no way.

With walls of water on either side the Israelites crossed through the dried-out seabed on dry ground.

Not long after, the Egyptians tried to cross the dried-out ocean floor in pursuit. Once the Israelites had crossed, however, God wreaked havoc with the Egyptian forces. He threw them into confusion and flicked the wheels off their chariots. Then he commanded Moses to once again stretch out his hand. The waters began to return to their normal place. Pharaoh and his forces tried to retreat, but they all drowned. '*Not one of them survived.*' (Exodus 14:28)

The Israelites then '*…feared the Lord and put their trust in him and in Moses his servant.*' (Exodus 14:31)

What we learn from this account is: The impossible and impassable are no obstacles for God. God can make a way where there is no way. He uses the supernatural to make the natural do his will and purpose. He is a God of purpose, power and love.

No matter what we're facing, we don't need to fear being trapped by our circumstances because God is our deliverer.

6

Being Afraid of God Rather than the Reverential Awe (Fear) of God

Exodus 20:18–21

A sixth reference in scripture to the words '*do not be afraid*' is found in Exodus 20:18–21 (cf. Deuteronomy 5:1–33; Hebrews 12:18–29). A little more detail than normal is added to accurately set the scene and describe (as best one can) what it must have been like for the Israelites to encounter the glory of the Lord. Let's use our imaginations to try and picture the scene.

The story takes place about three months after the Israelites have been set free from Egypt (Exodus 19:1). They are now on the other side of the Red Sea where they have camped in the desert at the base of Mt Sinai.

Mount Sinai

God summoned Moses up the mountain where he received a message for the people: '*You yourselves have seen what I did in Egypt, and how I carried you on eagles' wings and brought you to myself.*' (Exodus 19:4) What beautiful and reassuring words: '*I…brought you to myself.*'

God didn't deliver them out of Egypt just to bring them to a Promised Land, nor did he display his great power just to resettle them. He brought them out so they could be *with him*. This was profound.

God's whole motivation in everything he did for them was to bring them into a deeper level of relationship. The ultimate destination of their journey was not a place so much as a person—God himself.

Even though they had the visible signs of God's divine presence with them (pillar of cloud by day and pillar of fire by night), Mt Sinai was the climax of the journey. Until the Israelites entered into covenant they had not attained the fullness of relationship with God. So he brought them out to Mt Sinai to make himself known and to unfold his covenant.

As part of this dialogue, God told Moses that, if the Israelites would obey his covenant, then out of all the nations he would make them into his treasured possession—his exclusive people (Exodus 19:4). Moses returned to the people, summoned the elders and conveyed God's message. '*The people all responded together, "We will do everything the Lord has said."*' (Exodus 19:8)

After giving the Lord the people's response, Moses was commanded to prepare them through consecration.

In three days' time God was going to come down (Exodus 19:10–14). A clear decree proclaimed that access to the mountain and its surrounds was prohibited. Trespassing was to be punished by death. The mountain was to be set apart as holy (Exodus 19:12–13, 23).

Fearful sights and sounds

On the third day, the people woke to terrifying sights and sounds (Exodus 19:16–19). Mt Sinai was shrouded in a thick cloud. A ferocious inferno raged as dense smoke billowed up from the mountain. The people heard deafening, rumbling peels of thunder and witnessed blinding flashes of lightning. In addition, there were ear–shattering blasts of a trumpet which grew increasingly louder.

The mountain trembled violently like a localised seismic event. '*Then Moses spoke and the voice of the Lord answered with thunder.*' (Exodus 19:19; cf. Deuteronomy 5:4, 22). Amid this terrifying spectacle, the '*Lord descended to the top of Mount Sinai.*' (Exodus 19:20)

Chapter Six

Moses met with God before leading the people out of their camp to the foot of the mountain. Moses was then summoned onto the mountain where God reiterated the sacredness and sanctity of the sight. Upon his return, God spoke the words that we call the Ten Commandments.

> There is a huge difference between being afraid of God and fearing God.

Do not fear

This is where the reference to '*do not fear*' comes into focus. The sights and sounds of the glory, majesty and voice of God were more than the people could bear.

Exodus 20:18 states that the people '*...trembled with fear... [and] stayed at a distance...*' According to Deuteronomy 5: 23–27, the tribal leaders and elders were deputised to plead with Moses to pass on God's messages rather than hear God's voice for themselves out of fear they would die.

In fact, Hebrews 12:20 reveals that it wasn't the voice that was terrifying as much as what God said '*...they could not bear what was commanded: "If even an animal touches the mountain, it must be stoned."*' But they were, however, prepared to obey whatever God said (Deuteronomy 5:27).

Moses replied, '*Do not be afraid. God has come to test you, so that the fear of God will be with you to keep you from sinning.*' (Exodus 20:20)

The Israelites had the wrong fear of God. The people were afraid *of* God, whereas God's heart was that they would fear him in the sense of reverential awe and right living (Deuteronomy 5:29). The Lord wanted them to be his holy people by living a holy life.

God wanted them to lovingly and willingly relate to and obey him in covenant relationship. There is a huge difference between being afraid *of* God and *fearing* God.

To express his passion for his people, the Deuteronomy account of this event shows that, when God heard that the people wanted Moses to be their mediator, he said, '*I have heard what this people said to you. Everything they said was good.*' (Deuteronomy 5:28) Then came the cry of God's heart: '*Oh, that their hearts would be inclined to fear me and keep all my commands always, so that it might go well with them and their children forever.*' (Deuteronomy 5:29)

God gave them the commandments so they would know how to live a right, righteous and holy life. It was the prescribed way of living fully and freely. But God wanted them to obey him because in their hearts they revered and honoured him as their God, and not out of the fear of punishment. If they would obey from the heart, their lives would be blessed.

Testing

After Moses urged them not to be afraid, he gave an insight into the purpose of the divine manifestation on the mountain. '*God has come to test you, so that the fear of God will be with you to keep you from sinning.*' (Exodus 20:20)

Moses wanted this experience to be more than some overpowering emotion; he wanted it to be a motivating force for them to obey the law of God. He wanted this experience to not only cause awe, but to be a transforming attitude in changing their behaviour.

> Don't fear God's voice or his presence... live by his law and stay within the boundaries. Live as the people of God and he will be your God.

'*God has come to test you*' is suggestive of God testing Abraham: the fear of the Lord, the audible voice of God and the idea of testing (Genesis 22). As Abraham was about to plunge the knife into Isaac, the '*...angel of the Lord called out to him from heaven, "...Do not lay a hand on the boy. Do not do anything to him. Now I know that you fear God..."*' (Genesis 22:11–12)

So the clear purpose of the test was to see what was in Abraham's heart, whether or not he would obey God.

Similarly, the manifest demonstration of God's presence on the mountain was given as a test for obedience. Would the people obey the Covenant Code (Ten Commandments)? Would they live the way God wanted them to live?

By way of paraphrase, when Moses said, '*do not be afraid*,' his meaning ran along the lines of: 'Don't fear God's voice or his presence. Don't be afraid of the visible and audible manifestations of the power and glory of your God. He has come to test you—to see if you really will live as he wants you to live. He has come to see if you will fully and willingly obey him. Also, he has come to show you what kind of God he is. You saw his power in Egypt, but now you're seeing his glory and holiness. Therefore, let the reality of his holy presence motivate you to keep his commands, live by his law and stay within the boundaries. Live as the people of God and he will be your God.'

The Book of Hebrews contrasts Mt Sinai with Mt Zion

There is a startling New Testament and New Covenant parallel to this story in Hebrews 12:18–29. The author of Hebrews contrasts the Old Covenant to the superiority of the New Covenant.

Just as Moses was the mediator of the Old Covenant, so Jesus has become the mediator of the New Covenant. In verses 18–24, the author starkly contrasts the events at Mt Sinai with what the Lord has done for us (as his new covenant people) through Jesus (the mediator of the new covenant).

- We haven't come to tangible Mt Sinai; we have come to the heavenly Mt Zion (compare v. 18 with v. 22)
- We haven't come to fire, darkness, thunder, lightning, trumpets with fear of the divine presence, but we are now part of the community of the redeemed and are welcome in the divine presence (compare vv. 18–19 with v. 22)
- We are not filled with fear in the divine presence, but are filled with joy in the divine presence (compare vv. 20–21 with v. 22)

- We are not afraid to approach God but through the mediation of Jesus and his blood we can come close to him with boldness and confidence (compare v. 21 with v. 24).

But there is a sobering implication the author of Hebrews makes: '*See to it that you do not refuse him who speaks.*' (Hebrews 12:25) When God speaks to us, we must yield, respond and obey.

The author of Hebrews then outlined good reasons for responding appropriately to God's voice: '*…If they did not escape when they refused him who warned them on earth, how much less will we, if we turn away from him who warns us from heaven?*' (Hebrews 12:25)

The Exodus generation refused to listen to God and his Covenant Code. As a result, the entire generation was disqualified from entering the Promised Land. How much more should we respond in repentance, obedience or compliance when we too hear his voice, especially in Scripture. This is a warning not to be frivolous or flippant with the things of God or with the salvation we have received. This is a warning to be obedient to the Word of God and not treat it as some extraneous appendage to our lives. This is a warning not to quench the Spirit of God or treat him with disregard.

While emphasising and underlining that we do not need to be afraid of God, we must also retain a healthy fear of God.

Fear of the Lord

Throughout Scripture, the 'fear of the Lord' means to have an attitude of reverence and awe toward the Lord. 'Fearing' God, in this respect, comes from recognising and responding to him as the all–powerful, all–knowing, ever–present God whose Word is eternal truth.

A number of Scriptures give insight into the purpose and meaning of the fear of the Lord:
- Fear of the Lord is the '*beginning of knowledge* (wisdom)' (Proverbs 1:7) meaning that taking God and his Word into account is the foundation of a disciplined and holy life

Chapter Six

> The 'fear of the Lord' should guide us in the way we engage with him, live our lives, and conduct our relationships...

- Fear of the Lord means to adhere to and obey his Word—the prescribed way he wants us to live (Deuteronomy 13:4; Ecclesiastes 12:13)
- Fear of the Lord means to serve God exclusively and reject every other competing affection or deity (idol, god) (Deuteronomy 6:13; Joshua 24:14)
- Fear of the Lord is expressed by walking in his ways, loving him and serving him with all our heart and soul (Deuteronomy 10:12)
- Fear of the Lord means to recognise him as Creator and that his plans stand firm forever (Psalm 33:8–11)
- Fear of the Lord means to reject, shun and dispel evil (Proverbs 3:7; 8:13; 16:6) and so it should keep us from sinning
- Fear of the Lord should be a motivating force to live with an appropriate attitude of reverence toward him (1 Peter 1:17)
- Fear of the Lord should also be the motivation to live and work ethically and to exercise impartial justice (2 Chronicles 19:7)
- Fear (reverence) of God is the basis for our submissive attitudes toward 'authority' in the home and church (Ephesians 5:21)

There is a vast difference between the 'fear of the Lord' described above to the 'fear' Adam experienced after eating the forbidden fruit. Adam feared the consequences of his actions. He knew that God knew about his sin and would dispense punishment.

In contrast, the fear of the Lord is giving proper weight and recognition to God, his nature and Word as a motivating force in our lives to keep us from sinning, and to live responsibly and biblically. The 'fear of the Lord' should guide us in the way we engage with him, live our lives, and conduct our relationships in marriage, family, church and broader community.

The fear of the Lord should cause us to revere him, honour him, be in awe of Him, walk humbly before him, live right, live clean, live in purity, obey Him, and worship Him. Let's never be frivolous, blasé, or careless with the grace we have received through Jesus Christ.

God is a consuming fire

The author of Hebrews then went on to write that just as the Lord shook Mt Sinai, so he will '...*shake not only the earth but also the heavens.*' (Hebrews 12:26). Everything that is part of this visible creation will be shaken. This means it will be judged, assessed, appraised, rightly valued and made new.

His conclusion: '*Therefore, since we are receiving a kingdom that cannot be shaken, let us be thankful, and so worship God acceptably with reverence and awe, for our God is a consuming fire.*' (Hebrews 12:28–29) The Kingdom of God of which we are a part through Jesus Christ will not and cannot be shaken. Our salvation and eternity are secure.

To this, the author writes we should do two things: '*be thankful*' and '*worship God acceptably*'. In regard to thankfulness, we should be thankful for the new covenant, sonship as heirs of the Kingdom of God and our eternal hope and future.

One of the ways we express our thankfulness is through '*acceptable worship*'. True worship has little to do with a particular tradition or expression, whether Pentecostal or Liturgical. Songs, style, genre, volume or location are irrelevant. According to this verse, 'acceptable' worship comes from the attitude of our hearts being filled with reverence and awe. May we never forget the final words of this chapter (Hebrews 12) which are a direct quote from Deuteronomy 4:24: '*God is a consuming fire.*'

Drawing near to God

Before concluding this sobering chapter, let's quickly return to our original focus in Exodus 20 to make one final application. In verse 21, we read that because of fear the '... *people remained at a distance, while Moses approached the thick darkness where God was.*'

Sadly, a lot of people in our churches live like the Israelites—they '... *remain at a distance*'. They are like the elders of Israel and ask their ministers and leaders, 'You pray for me...you hear from God for me.' This is primarily because they know what is in their hearts. Rather than come closer to God by dealing with things in their lives, they stay at a content and comfortable distance.

> Through the new covenant God welcomes and invites us to come as we are with all our faults, frailties and fears.

Through the new covenant, however, God welcomes and invites us to come as we are with all our faults, frailties and fears. Through Jesus, he will never reject us, never turn his back on us and never forsake us. By his grace, we have complete acceptance (Acts 15:11; Romans 3:24; Titus 3:7). By his blood, we have bold, unhindered access to him anywhere and at any time (Hebrews 10:19–22; Ephesians 3:12). By the indwelling of the Holy Spirit, we have his divine presence within us (John 14:17; 1 Corinthians 3:16; 6:19).

Therefore, let's not stay at a distance because of fear—God already knows what is in our heart. Rather, by his grace to us through Christ Jesus, let's come close, live right, live according to holy law (beatitudes and the Scriptural way to live), honour him, please him, adore him, pursue him, desire him, love him, cry out to him, and draw close to him. We should be like Moses who '...*approached...where God was.*'

Let's not live in the live in fear of God's vengeance, punishment, rejection or wrath, but through Jesus revere him as a gracious, merciful, accepting and loving God.

7

Fear of Change

Deuteronomy 31:6

Mark Twain is said to have once quipped that the 'only person who likes change is a baby with a wet diaper'. Change is uncomfortable. Change is unsettling. Change is confronting.

Importantly, in the Christian life and church–life, change is inevitable and inescapable. Change makes some people fearful. The attitude we adopt in navigating change is the determining factor in whether we defeat the fear of change or not.

Some people, however, have the naïve view that change is instant as the following (tongue–in–cheek) story illustrates. A couple who lived in outback Queensland had a daughter about to be married. Being their only child, they drove her 2,000 kilometers to the capital city, Brisbane, to buy her an exquisite wedding dress from the city's most exclusive store. None of them had ever ventured into the 'big smoke' before so they were awestruck by the freeways, skyscrapers and dense traffic. Eventually, they came to the large building in which the wedding store was located. Unable to find parking, the father dropped his wife and daughter off but gave them clear instructions, 'I'll look for a parking spot. Have a good look in the shop. If you find one, then please call me and I'll come as soon as I can.'

The mother and daughter walked into the ground floor entry area of the building, completely overwhelmed by the size and opulence of the décor. An attendant at the Information Counter courteously informed them that the store they sought was on the 7th floor. She pointed to the elevators on the far side. They had never seen a lift before. To them, they just looked like shiny metal doors with a series of illuminated numbers above them. Cautiously and slowly they made their way over to the elevator doors not really knowing what to do. To their surprise the doors opened. Their eyes grew wide and their mouths dropped. Still and speechless, they peered in.

As they stood gazing into the lift, a gruff middle–aged man slovenly walked past them and entered the lift. He stunk of foul body odour. He was dishevelled, his hair unkempt and his ill–fitting clothes were dreadfully out of fashion. His hairy belly button was partially exposed because his shirt wasn't tucked in far enough. He saw them looking at him and gave a creepy smile exposing his yellow teeth, many of which were missing. They winced in repulsion. Mercifully the doors closed, but they couldn't take their eyes off the doors.

Several moments later the same doors reopened. The shabby man was no longer there. Instead there was an incredibly handsome young man in his early thirties. He was dressed and groomed impeccably and tastefully. His physique showed that he was in excellent physical condition. As he walked out of the lift he, too, saw the two ladies staring at him. Being accustomed to ladies' attention, he smiled and nodded respectfully while greeting them with the single word, 'Ladies!' Their knees nearly gave way. After a few silent moments, the mother looked at the lift, then back at her daughter, before once again staring back at the lift. 'Quick,' she instructed her daughter, 'go and get your father.'

> Change is not something we need to fear. Rather, if it is God–initiated, it is something to embrace.

Like the 'mother' in this amusing story, many people think change is an easy, sudden or automatic process. Simply walk into the lift, the doors will close and 'presto' change will happen. Change is not like that. It is a slow process. But change is not something we need to fear. Rather, if it is God–initiated, it is something to embrace.

In this chapter, we'll explore a story in Scripture where people had to face *change* despite their fear that the future would be uncertain. The broader story is found in Deuteronomy 31:1–6, but the reference to *'do not fear'* is found in verse 6.

Moses' imminent death

In the last chapter, we left the Israelites at the base of Mt Sinai entering into Covenant relationship with the LORD. Tragically, from this high point, they nose–dived into failure, disobedience and rebellion. Consequently, the whole Exodus generation forfeited the Promised Land.

However, during the subsequent forty years wandering in the wilderness, a new generation had emerged. In the immediate context, they're camped in the desert on the east of the Jordan River. Moses had just finished his verbal reflection of the Exodus generation's journey and the reiteration of the Covenant Code and Mosaic Law.

Then came a very poignant moment. Moses said, '*I am now one hundred and twenty years old and I am no longer able to lead you. The Lord has said to me, "You shall not cross the Jordan."*' (Deuteronomy 31:2)

Moses conceded he was old and physically incapable of leading them any longer. He also confessed he had been forbidden to enter the Promised Land.

It is not stated, but implied, that Moses' words sent shock waves through his listeners that day. Moses was the only leader they had ever known. He was the one who had been God's mouthpiece and their mediator. Now he disclosed he would not be leading them into the Promised Land. The people were on the borders of a land they had never ventured into. The future was the great unknown.

They'd had a pillar of cloud by day and pillar of fire by night, but all that was about to change—things would be vastly different than they'd ever known before. Without Moses they would be facing the occupying nations alone. They had never journeyed into the unchartered without Moses leading them, and they had never faced battles this big without his godly leadership.

From Moses' words in Deuteronomy 31:3–6, we can deduce that the people were feeling vulnerable, insecure and uncertain about the future without him leading them.

Likewise, there are times in our Christian journey when change occurs and challenges come. For example, it may be a change of home, job, career, pastor or church. Some of these changes are the result of our own choices, but some happen beyond our control.

> Change is a transitional point between where we have been and where he wants us to be... remember that God is waiting for us on the other side.

We realise that life is never going to be the same again. Maybe like the Israelites, we feel vulnerable, insecure or intimidated by the changes we are facing. If so, we need to apply Moses' words to the Israelites for ourselves.

There is a hint that Moses anticipated the people's natural fears and uncertainties, so he gave them a number of pre–emptive assurances. His words were designed to gird them against the fears which 'change' may spawn. We'll work through each of his words and make an application to our lives.

God himself would cross over ahead of them (Deut. 31:3a)

Moses firstly encouraged them with the words, '*The Lord your God himself will cross over ahead of you.*' (Deuteronomy 31:3a)

God would be intimately intertwined in their future as much as he had been involved in their past. The future was the next step in their ongoing journey toward possessing the promises God had given Moses and their forefathers. The Lord assured them he would *'cross over ahead'* of them. He would go before them. He was not asking them to go anywhere or to do anything without the absolute certainty of his constant presence. As he had been in the past, he would be in the future.

> God is the God of our future, not just our past.
>
> He knows the future.
>
> He knows where he's leading us.

Lessons: God is the God of our future, not just our past. He knows the future. He knows where he's leading us. He has planned what he wants to do in us and through us (Ephesians 2:10).

Change is a transitional point (juncture) between where we have been and where he wants us to be. Whenever we are faced with change, we must remember that God is waiting for us on the other side. He's already there. He has been with us on the journey (even in the wilderness), he'll be with us through the process of change (no matter how uncomfortable and confronting), and he'll be on the other side of change ready to lead us further. Change is not something to fear because we know God is on the other side of it.

God himself would remove all obstacles and obstructions through them (Deut. 31:3b)

Moses then stated a second reassurance: God would *'cross over ahead'* of the people to *'destroy'* the inhabiting nations. (Deuteronomy 31:3b)

These nations were the cause and embodiment of the people's fear[10] and the major obstacle (in their minds) to possessing the land. Moses assured

---

10 Moses specifically said in v. 6, '*...Do not be afraid or terrified because of them...*' identifying the source of their fear as the inhabiting nations.

the people the Lord would clear the way for them to possess the land he had promised them.

To reinforce his point, Moses reminded them (in verse 4) of what the Lord had done to the Amorite kings, Sihon[11] and Og[12], when they resisted and obstructed the Israelites as they sojourned toward the Promised Land. Moses reassured them that what God had done to these two kings during the Exodus would also be done to the inhabiting peoples during the conquest.

On two occasions in his discourse, Moses emphasized that the Lord would fight *for* his people, but he would not do it alone. He would fight *with* his people, ensuring they would be triumphant.

In Deuteronomy 31:4, Moses said that the LORD would destroy the nations '*before*' them, implying they would be defeated in battle as the Israelites advanced. Moses also said, '*The Lord will deliver them to you, and you must do to them all that I have commanded you.*' (Deuteronomy 31:5)

The people would still have to fight, but God would bring the victory.

Lessons: There can be things in our own lives which are the personalised equivalents of the nations living in the Promised Land. These are the vulnerable areas of our lives which cause us to fear 'change'. As we have seen, in the fight against fear there is something we must do and something only God can do. Therefore the way by which we gain victory is by resisting fear *and* by trusting in the Lord's enabling and empowering to win the battle *through* us. He fights for us *by* fighting with us and through us.

God himself would fulfil his promises (Deut. 31:3c)

The third statement by Moses should have dispelled all the people's fear. Because God would cross over before them to drive out the opposing peoples, he declared: '*you will take possession of their land.*' (Deuteronomy. 31:3c)

---

11   The story of the Israelites defeating Sihon is found in Numbers 21:21–30; cf. Deuteronomy 2:24–35. It was so significant that the people of Jericho knew about it (Joshua 2:10) and Jephthah used Sihon's defeat as evidence to the king of Amorites of the Lord's power to deliver (Judges 11:19–22).
12   Og's defeat is located in Numbers 21:33–35.

They did not need to fear 'change' once Moses was no longer with them because God would fulfil his promise to give his people a land of their own where they would live as his exclusive people.

Lessons: God is faithful. God keeps his word. God fulfils his promises. God does what he says he will do. Therefore, we must trust God in times of change, even though the outcome maybe uncertain or unclear. We must believe God even though the process of 'change' is unsettling and uncomfortable.

'Change' is not something to fear because God uses it to align us with his purposes and conform us to his will. His ultimate intention in doing so is to bring us to the place where he can fulfil his promises to us.

God himself will provide people to guide and lead us through the process of change (Deut. 31:3d)

Moses' admission that he would no longer lead them evidently made the people feel insecure and vulnerable. However he added that *'Joshua also will cross over ahead of you...'* (Deuteronomy 31:3d)

They did not need to fear 'change' because, fourthly, God would appoint and affirm a new leader whose clear mandate and mission was to conquer and settle the people in the land of promise.

Lessons: The Lord will always position people in our lives to guide and encourage us in seasons of change. We are never alone in the process of change, even though it feels so lonely. Our sense of exposure is heightened in times of change, but the Lord will always bring the right people at the right time with the right experience to keep us moving forward.

Be strong and courageous

Moses concluded this defining moment with the exhortation: *'Be strong and courageous. Do not be afraid or terrified because of them, for the Lord your God goes with you; he will never leave you nor forsake you.'* (Deuteronomy 31:6)

After making the four assurances we have just explored, Moses urged them to respond in an appropriately positive and prophetic way as follows:

First, they had to '*be strong and courageous*'. The word '*be*' strong and courageous implies it was a choice, an intentional attitude they had to adopt. *Being* strong and courageous is a mindset which enables us to make right choices.

In times of change, we must choose to rise to the challenges before us with boldness and bravery, and respond to the uncertainties with fortitude and inward determination.

It's said: 'courage is not the absence of fear, but the mastery of it.' Another popular quote says that: 'courage is fear that has said its prayers.'

Do not be afraid

Secondly, on the basis of being strong and courageous, Moses instructed: '*Do not be afraid or terrified because of them…*'

We've already identified 'them' as a reference to the inhabiting nations in the promised Land. Phrased differently, the people must choose *not* to be afraid of facing the source and cause of their fears.

What does this mean for us?

- We must not be overcome by our insecurities
- We must not be afraid of what God has told us not to be afraid of
- We must guard our thoughts from succumbing to anxiety or fretting in times of change

There will be battles, challenges, obstacles, resistance and confronting moments, but we must not allow fear to dictate or determine the spiritual or emotional state of our lives.

He will never leave you nor forsake you

Moses then explicitly told the people why they shouldn't mindlessly surrender to fear and terror: '*…for the Lord your God goes with you.*' The Presence of the Lord God Almighty—the one who delivered them from the mighty power of Egypt—would be with them on the journey through change.

He was the God who brought them through an impassable sea, who decimated every force that resisted them on the journey, and who remained faithful when their forefathers were unfaithful. He revealed himself as a God whose 'word' and 'promises' can be trusted.

Likewise, there is a Presence with us on our journey in this life through moments of change. The Lord Jesus, whose Spirit indwells us, is with us every step of the way. He has promised he will bring us through anything and everything so his purposes and plans can be fulfilled. We are his people; he is our God. He is leading us; we are following.

> We do not need to fear 'change' because the Lord promises his abiding presence in times of insecurity.

Moses concluded his monologue by stating the undergirding and unshakable foundation of all his words: '*He will never leave you, nor forsake you.*' (Deuteronomy 31:6; cf. Hebrews 13:5)

The people would never be alone and would never be abandoned. Equally, we don't need to give any place to fear, fretting or anxiety because of change since in Christ we are never alone and we will never be abandoned.

Finally, the people were commanded not to fear change, but to adopt a resolute attitude because the change of leaders signalled the first steps in moving into their destiny—the land that God had promised the Patriarchs. In our lives, change need not contain or constrain us or cause us to fear. On the contrary, we've seen from this biblical reference that, *if* we respond appropriately, change will reposition and renew our lives in preparation for God's future purposes.

Above all, this chapter has taught us that we can fearproof our lives by resting in his accompanying, all–protective, ever–present, enduring presence. We do not need to fear 'change' because the Lord promises his abiding presence in times of insecurity.

8

Fear We Haven't Got What It Takes to Do What God Has Called Us to Do

Deuteronomy 31:7–8

Back in 1999, I was very busy in ministry with a number of demanding roles, but in my heart I was feeling unsettled and under-challenged. Change was coming.

Around the middle of the year, I was approached by a large church in Brisbane's southern suburbs to explore my willingness to be considered as one of the candidates for their new senior pastor. Because we were exploring a number of options at the time, I agreed to submit my name. After a long process their board unanimously offered me the role. The Lord clearly confirmed this step was his will.

The church had been through an inordinate amount of trauma over the years, so there was a detectable undercurrent of resistance and mistrust. At 37, I was the first younger pastor they'd had for a generation. The whole prospect and language of generational renewal and change brought insecurity and resistance.

The staff I inherited was capable but generally older than me. The church was filled with great people and a refreshing number of young people, but the sum total of the challenges listed above (and these were only a few) meant I had a huge job cut out for me to reinvent and reposition the church.

Even though I had an unmistakable sense of call, an incredible excitement about the future and a huge vision burning in my heart, I was not prepared for the crippling sense of inadequacy I felt within weeks. It overwhelmed me for months until I slowly began to apply the lessons I'll share in this chapter.

Maybe, like me, you have felt or do feel a sense of inadequacy about what God has called you to do. A sense of inadequacy fuels the fear that we haven't got what it takes to do what God has called us to do. This fear subsequently discourages, disempowers or disables us. We become inept and ineffective. God does not want us to respond to his call upon our lives with inadequacy and fear. Instead, he wants us to embrace our call with courage and conviction.

We see this illustrated in our eighth reference to *'do not fear'* which is found in Deuteronomy 31:7–8 (cf. Joshua 1:1–9). It comes immediately after the one we looked at in the previous chapter. These words became my theme during the first year of my tenure in the Brisbane church.

Brief background

Let's set the scene. Moses had gathered the people on the eastern side of the Jordan River. He had just revealed that he would not be crossing over with the Israelites into the Promised Land. After a number of reassuring promises, Moses stated that Joshua would be their new leader.

Moses then summoned Joshua and commissioned him in the presence of the people. This is where we read the next mention of *'do not fear'*:

> *'Be strong and courageous, for you must go with this people into the land that the Lord swore to their forefathers to give them, and you must divide it among them as their inheritance. The Lord himself goes before*

*you and will be with you; he will never leave you nor forsake you. **Do not be afraid**; do not be discouraged'* (Deuteronomy 31:7–8 emphasis mine).

Be strong and courageous

After Moses' death, Joshua was commissioned with a clear mandate to courageously assume leadership of the people and boldly lead them to conquer and possess the land (Joshua 1:6–9). Armed with the knowledge of the purpose of God and the promise of his continual presence, Joshua was commanded to be strong and courageous in discharging this call.

> Joshua not only knew God's call on his life, but he had to respond by having the right internal, mental and spiritual attitude toward it.

The words *'be strong and courageous'* would become a recurring theme (Deuteronomy 31:7–8, 23; Joshua 1:6–9).

God knew the challenges Joshua would face far exceeded his ability and would stretch him in every way. Joshua would need to have a daily dependence on the Presence of God.

So the Lord commanded him to maintain inward strength and outward courage. He must be fortified internally and bold externally. Joshua must not allow fear to hamstring or stifle the purpose of God for or through him. He must not be frozen by fear or disabled by discouragement. All of his life had been a preparation for this hour. Now, Joshua had to inwardly respond by adopting the right attitude.

There is an important lesson for each of us in God's command to Joshua to be strong and courageous. Joshua not only knew God's call on his life, but he had to respond by having the right internal, mental and spiritual attitude toward it. This was the only way Joshua could subdue fear and silence any sense of inadequacy he may have felt.

Joshua's possible predisposition

There are plausible hints that Joshua may have been vulnerable and predisposed towards fear, discouragement or feelings of inadequacy. This is suggested by the number of times the Lord had to command him to be 'strong and courageous', and by the reassuring language God used.

- Maybe Joshua had great faith in God, but doubted his own adequacy for the task
- Maybe Joshua was comfortable taking and obeying orders as a number two, but felt unprepared to assume the next level of leadership
- Maybe Joshua was wrestling with what was required of him to be *the* leader, so he waivered in his willingness
- Maybe past battles had taken their toll on Joshua emotionally and/or physically, so the prospect of further opposition and confrontation made him wince
- Maybe the prospect of taking over the leadership from an unparalleled leader like Moses caused Joshua to be (understandably) insecure

This is only speculative because no–one knows for sure, but each of us can probably identify with one or more of these responses.

Application

Like Joshua, there are seasons in our lives when God begins to do something new *within* us in preparation for him doing something new *through* us.

The Holy Spirit initiates a stirring in our hearts. Embers begin to fan into flame. Latent gifting starts to surface. Spiritual passion ignites within our hearts. A vision is revived within us. God begins to move in our life in new and unexpected ways.

Perhaps God has put a call upon our heart to:

- Care for orphans in the developing world
- Write or produce powerful dramas that will communicate spiritual truth

- Lead a Life Group that will reproduce itself and raise up leaders
- Raise large sums of money to finance missions' endeavours
- Produce cutting edge TV programs that portray Christian values
- Influence others in our profession or industry for his glory
- Intercede for the lost
- Sow our life and ministry as a missionary in a nation of the world
- Serve in the church or in leadership

On occasions, we may feel like Joshua—even though we have a clear and compelling sense of commission, we feel smothered or plagued by a sense of inadequacy. If so, then please note the following:

If you feel…	*Remember…*
Inadequate	God will empower you to do what he's called you to do
Fearful	God is fearless (afraid of nothing) and, by his Spirit, can enable you to overcome fear
Vulnerable	God will never leave you nor forsake you
Alone	God will be with you always
Prone to discouragement	God is your constant encourager
Uncertain about what the future may hold	God goes ahead of you and is with you on the journey
Insecure about whether you have what it takes	God has called you and gives you the grace and gifting to do what he's called you to do
Afraid that if you step out you'll be misunderstood and ridiculed	Jesus was misunderstood and ridiculed so you can draw strength from him

As we have seen throughout this book, in the fight against fear there is something God will do and something we must do. In the particular fight against inadequacy, we see these two elements in Joshua's example.

God's role

We note God's role through his words to Joshua (which I'll paraphrase from Joshua 1:1–9):

'Joshua (insert your name), yesterday's gone. Everything you've been through your whole life has been preparation for this hour. I have called you. I have revealed to you my specific will. I will enable you. I will protect you. I will give you a sense of my conscious presence. I will give you the fulfilment of the promises. I will be with you wherever you go. Feed upon and follow my Word continually and wholeheartedly. Now, step into your ministry. Lead boldly. Do not allow yourself to fall victim to terror or discouragement.'

> Our role, in response to God's initiative, is to be strong and courageous... we must not allow fear or discouragement to paralyse us.

In summary, God initiated the call, gave Joshua the capacity to lead and promised his presence as he did so.

Our role

Our role, in response to God's initiative, is to *be* strong and courageous. How can we be strong and courageous? By adopting the right inward attitude of fortitude and boldness.

Despite our natural disposition, we must *not* allow fear or discouragement to paralyse us. Instead, we must embrace an attitude of determination. We must resolve to do what God has called us to do.

In concluding this chapter, let me return to my Brisbane experience. It took many months of meditating on these very words before I was able to master the sense of inadequacy. I had occasional setbacks, especially after difficult times, but I progressively grew in confidence and courage as a leader.

Just as Joshua (and me to a far lesser degree) stepped into leadership, may we be encouraged to step up to what God is calling us to do:

- Initiate and implement change in our lives
- Believe for new dimensions
- Pray big, adventurous and audacious prayers
- Pursue God–given, unfulfilled dreams
- Follow the leading of the Holy Spirit
- Deal with opposition and negativity around us
- Take decisive steps of obedient faith
- Make adjustments when we are wrong
- Selflessly make sacrifices and pay whatever price is necessary
- Boldly step into our God–filled future and fulfil your commission.

9

Fear that Past Failures Will Hinder Our Future Successes

Joshua 8:1–2

Everyone has secrets. What is the last thing in the world you would want people to know about you? It's what we do with those secrets that determine their effect upon our lives. If we disclose them to God and the appropriate people, the ramifications are vastly reduced. But if we conceal them, we'll inevitably discover that hidden secrets have consequences.

The disastrous consequences of burying secrets are powerfully portrayed in our ninth reference to the command '*do not fear*' which is found in Joshua 8:1–2.

Background of Joshua 8

In our journey, we've now entered a new phase in Old Testament history called the Conquest, when the children of Israel began to 'take' the land.

Moses had died (Joshua 1:1) and, as we saw in the last chapter, Joshua had been commissioned to boldly and courageously lead the Israelites (Joshua 1:2–9). Under his leadership, the Israelites had miraculously crossed over the flooded Jordan river on dry ground (Joshua 3:17).

They were now poised and positioned on the eastern border of the 'Promised Land'.

In the story preceding our reference, the people had witnessed an incredible display of divine power as God brought down the impregnable and imposing walls of Jericho (Joshua 6). This was their first victory *in* possessing the Promised Land.

Ai—an anatomy of defeat (Josh. 7: 2-5)
But in the very next battle, Israel experienced a resounding defeat (Joshua 7: 2–5). The town of Ai was much smaller, and an easier target than the large and well-defended Jericho.

A relatively small force of about 3,000 went up to take Ai, but they were humiliatingly defeated. At least 36 men lost their lives. Consequently, '... *the people melted and became like water.*' (Joshua 7:5)

What went wrong? Initially Joshua did the correct strategic thing by sending spies to do some reconnaissance (Joshua 7:2). As on a previous occasion, the spies, however, were not the best indicator. Their reports could be paraphrased: 'It's a piece of cake. We don't even need the whole army, just send a small battalion.'

The people relied on the spies and did not carefully plan the battle, nor seek the support of the Lord.

Suffering the sting of defeat, Joshua and the leaders went into mourning. Joshua tore his clothes and fell facedown to the ground before the ark of the Lord. The elders did the same thing and sprinkled dust on their heads to signify their woe. Joshua was concerned about the reputation of the people and the Lord so he cried out in concern and lament.

Basically, he cried out, 'God, why? You are supposed to be Israel's divine warrior, so why were we defeated? Why didn't you fight for us as you did at Jericho?'

'*If only we had been content to stay on the other side of the Jordan?*' (Joshua 7:7)

Difference between Jericho and Ai

What was the big difference between Jericho and Ai?

The Lord answered Joshua's bellyache by saying, 'On your feet, Joshua. Stop your lamenting! Don't you blame me for this catastrophe or defeat. Joshua, it is Israel who has sinned for "...*they have violated my covenant, which I commanded them to keep. They have taken some of the devoted things; they have stolen, they have lied, they have put them with their own possessions.*" That's the problem!'

Here in Joshua 7:11, God explains *why* Israel had been in defeat and retreat.

The reason was that one man, Achan—whose name means '*trouble*' or '*troublesome*'—from the tribe of Judah, had coveted and stolen some of the spoils of Jericho. God had clearly told them that everything in Jericho was to be destroyed—there was to be no plunder. But Achan had smuggled out a Babylonian robe, 200 shekels of silver and a wedge of gold and had hidden them in the ground inside his tent (Joshua 7:21).

The defeat at Ai signalled that something was wrong in the war camp, so the Lord revealed to Joshua *why* Israel had been defeated. Someone had violated the command of the Lord.

The personal sin of Achan had consequences upon the whole community which was being held back from further progress and conquest.

Exposure and confession

In Joshua 7:12–13, the Lord revealed, '*I will not be with you any more unless you destroy whatever among you is devoted to destruction...You cannot stand against your enemies until you remove it.*' In other words, 'You are not going to progress any further or take any more ground *until* you deal with what is hidden and uncover buried secrets.'

Not only did the Lord name their sin, but he demanded cleansing: '*Go consecrate the people. Tell them, "Consecrate yourselves in preparation for tomorrow..."*' (Joshua 7:13) A holy God demands a holy people, so he showed Joshua how to discover the sinner.

Next morning, the people filed past Joshua tribe by tribe, clan by clan, household by household until, eventually, Achan was exposed.

Joshua confronted Achan who openly confessed and revealed the secret location where the goods were hidden. Men were dispatched to bring the concealed booty. Joshua, together with all the people, took Achan, his plunder, his entire household and his livestock—all that he had—to the valley of Achor.

What was Joshua going to do with the secret that had been uncovered in the people? Before we look at the answer to that question, let's explore the relevance of this story to our lives.

Application to our lives

Achan had something forbidden in his life that was hidden and buried. He had a secret nobody else knew. He had *knowingly* violated a clear command from God. However, because it was discreetly hidden, Achan mistakenly believed his actions would never be uncovered.

But Achan could never have foreseen his individual deed of covetousness would have such disastrous consequences for the whole community, especially his family.

The Israelites experienced *defeat* at Ai because of his selfish act (coveting) and subsequent actions (covering).

> Secrets show scorn and contempt for God, whereas God wants our life to honour and reverentially fear him.

Like Achan, everybody has secrets. The big question we must ask ourselves is whether, in the eyes of God, our secrets are hidden and buried *or* open and exposed? Like Achan, we'll discover that secrets have consequences. Therefore, another big question is whether we'll uncover our secrets to the grace and mercy of God or bury them deeper and suffer their toxic corrosion in our lives?

Chapter Nine

Danger of secrets

Secrets show scorn and contempt for God, whereas God wants our life to honour and reverentially fear him. Secrets belong to the realm of darkness, lies and deception, whereas God wants our lives to be full of light, truth and transparency. Secrets are areas in our lives which remain unexposed to the light of God's grace, whereas he wants to bring people to true repentance and forgiveness. Secrets bind us up on the inside and affect our lives, whereas God wants his people to be inwardly untangled and free from ongoing residue.

God's heart is for his people to be free from all the noxious effects of secrets such as:

- Regret and baggage
- Unconfessed and unforgiven sin
- Bitterness and brokenness
- Distrust and mistrust
- Disbelief and unbelief
- Hopelessness and emptiness
- Guilt and shame

The Lord wants us to be free from every limitation so we can grow in intimacy with him, in Christlikeness of character, and in wholeness and holiness. He desires that we live with transparency and authenticity.

This is the only way he can fulfil his purposes *in* and *through* our lives, and be *all* that God created and redeemed us to be.

God wants to take us to new heights and depths in his purposes, but many people have internal barriers and blockages caused by unseen, unclean

> God's grace can reach into the darkest recesses of our hearts to give us the resolve and strength we need.

and unexposed *secrets*. If we are to move forward, we need to let God *deal* with them.

What should we do with our hidden secrets?

Ultimately we have to make a choice about our hidden secrets—will we deal with them before God with an open heart? Or will we refuse to do so by hardening our hearts?

My heartfelt encouragement, though, is to honestly, openly and courageously uncover them to God's grace.

1. Ask the Lord for his mercy and grace

Sometimes we don't deal with our secrets because they're too painful, shameful or confrontational. God's grace can reach into the darkest recesses of our hearts to give us the resolve and strength we need. He will equip us not only to face but to work through the consequences of our secrets.

The author of Hebrews wrote about how Jesus, our great High Priest, identifies and sympathises with our human frailty and weaknesses. On that basis he exhorted: *'Let us then approach the throne of grace with confidence, so that we may receive mercy and find grace to help us in our time of need.'* (Hebrews 4:16)

The first principle here is to unashamedly *'approach the throne of grace'* through prayer and confidently and expectantly ask for *'mercy and grace'*. Ask!

2. Acknowledgment and confession to God

The next step is to fully acknowledge and confess the secret to God (1 John 1:9). Please don't minimise, trivialise or rationalise the secret, but humbly, honestly and fully disclose it to God. *'...he who conceals his sins does not prosper, but whoever confesses and renounces them finds mercy.'* (Proverbs 28:13)

Confession brings the secret into the *light*. Darkness cannot remain where there is light. Yield the secret things to Jesus and ask for his forgiveness and cleansing. As we do so, the light of the Spirit's presence will probe and purify our heart.

Like David, whose adulterous and murderous secret had been exposed by the prophet Nathan (2 Samuel 12:1–12), we must turn to God in confession (2 Samuel 12:13).

David more fully elaborated on the acknowledgment of his sin by writing a prayer for God's mercy (Psalm 51: 1). This powerful Psalm clearly shows David's depth of repentance (vv. 3–6) and contrition (v. 17). He pleaded for mercy (v. 1), to be cleansed to the roots (vv. 7–9) and for renewal (v. 10). David cried out for inner transformation.

If we don't know how to seek for the Lord's forgiveness through confession, let's seek the guidance of someone wise, trustworthy and spiritual.

3. Bravely face the consequences
Concealed secrets always have consequences.

God is a merciful, forgiving and just God. Through the cross we can find immediate, complete and assured cleansing from any and all sin. There are times, however, when there are consequences for our actions.

By way of example, if there has been infidelity, the betrayed spouse may *forgive* the offending partner, but it will take a very long time to re-establish *trust*. This is a consequence the sinning partner will have to face.

Another instance may be a marriage that is chronically unhappy, but a well-disguised secret. No one else may ever suspect. By his grace, the Lord can give the couple a capacity and hope for a happy marriage, but *they* must work through the causes and consequences. It will be a long road, but well worth it.

> We must not misinterpret the consequences of sin as punishment from God. We reap what we have sown.

A third common example is when a person, normally a male, confesses to a problem with pornography. Even though he may have 'confessed' and demonstrated genuine contrition, there will have to be preventative measures put in place, such as appropriate software and personal accountability, to reduce future temptations.

We must not misinterpret the *consequences* of sin as punishment from God. God is gracious and does not treat us as our sins deserve (Psalm 103:10), but there is a principle in creation called 'sowing and reaping'. We reap what we have sown. There is cause and effect.

Bravely do what you need to do to find wholeness, reconciliation, restitution, discipline or deliverance. It would be foolish and naïve to say it will be easy to work through some of the consequences. It will take courage, resolve and determination, but it is liberating to find true freedom by uncovering secrets.

Achan's judgment

Joshua had to deal with the 'secret' which had been exposed in the people. Some pages ago, we left Achan, his family and possessions standing in the valley of Achor awaiting sentencing.

The judgment was commensurate with the crime. *'Then all Israel stoned him, and after they stoned the rest, they burned them. Over Achan they heaped up a large pile of rocks, which remains to this day. Then the Lord turned from his fierce anger…'* (Joshua 7:25–26)

Similarly, like Joshua and the children of Israel, we must be ruthless with the 'Achans' (secrets) in our lives. We must repent and ask the Lord's forgiveness for burying things in our lives. We need to prayerfully expose them to his mercy and grace as we seek for complete cleansing.

A big lesson

Joshua did not know they were vulnerable or unprotected until they experienced the unexpected defeat at Ai and sought the Lord to find out why. Likewise, Samson did not know that the Spirit of the Lord had departed from him until he was overpowered by the Philistines.

Equally, some people who live with 'Achan' secrets rarely know something is wrong *until* they are spiritually attacked or in spiritual bondage. Reflect on the following statements to see if any are applicable:

- Satan is attacking me and I can never seem to get victory
- I feel besieged by the powers of darkness
- I cannot (or no longer) hear the voice of God
- I have no consciousness of the Lord's presence any longer
- I read the Scriptures but they seem dry or dead

If any of these are relevant, maybe God wants to deal with something hidden in your life. We may need the light of the Spirit of God to expose the 'Achan' secrets in us. We need to ask ourselves:

- What legal right does Satan have to attack me?
- What ground have I unintentionally or inadvertently given him?
- How have I failed to deal with something as prescribed in the Word of God?
- Is there something I have withheld from God?
- Have I been completely obedient with what God told me to deal with?
- Is there something 'hidden' in my life which gives Satan influence?

When the Holy Spirit exposes what we have concealed, we must respond in contrition and confession. By doing so, God will shed his light and love on our lives and break the strongholds of secrecy once and for all.

Do not fear

So far in this chapter we have not actually addressed the reference to '*do not fear*', but this is where it comes into focus.

Achan and his household had been purged from the people, but the problematic city of Ai had not yet been taken. At this point, the Lord said to Joshua, '*Do not be afraid; do not be discouraged. Take the whole army with you, and go up and attack Ai. For I have delivered into your hands the king of Ai, his people, his city and his land.*' (Joshua 8:1)

> We are not defined by our past; we are defined by God's future purposes for us in Christ Jesus.

It seems that Joshua was wrestling with the fear that past failures will hinder future successes. But God's words in Joshua 8:1–2 reassured him he would experience victory. In essence, the Lord said, 'You've tasted defeat, but you have learnt from it. The lessons from defeat will assure you of future victory. Now that you've put things right, you will succeed.'

If we've failed or experienced defeat—maybe through a hidden secret—we need to go and put things right. Once we've done so, we no longer need to be afraid or discouraged. Learning the lessons of past failures assures us of future successes. Our past doesn't hinder our future unless we fail to deal with it. Instead, if we deal with it, God will reposition and redeploy us for victory. We are not defined by our past; we are defined by God's future purposes for us in Christ Jesus.

Outcome of the story

Armed with an assurance of victory and divinely-given strategies, Joshua mobilised the army to attack Ai. This time, however, they were allowed to keep the plunder.

The ambushes were successful, so the Israelite forces decimated Ai's residents and structures. '*So Joshua burned Ai and made it a permanent heap of ruins, a desolate place to this day.*' (Joshua 8:28).

10

Fear of Being Rejected Because of How We See Ourselves

Judges 6:23

This may come as a surprise about a preacher, but I really enjoy science fiction films (unless they're scary, sexy or gory). I love going to a galaxy far, far away to encounter extra–terrestrial life forms. As a teenager, I remember the original *Star Wars* film as part of the first trilogy. The spacecraft and special effects captured my young imagination.

Many years later, filmmaker George Lucas produced another trilogy which chronologically preceded the first three and gave insights into the origins of the saga's characters and story. One of the interesting twists over the trilogy was the evolution of the heroic young boy Anakin Skywalker into the evil dark lord—Darth Vader.

An ingenious advertising poster for the first of these films, *The Phantom Menace,* showed a very young Anakin Skywalker standing in front of a dwelling. His shadow, however, morphed into the shape of Darth Vader. It gave viewers an insight into what this young boy would become later in his life. It creatively showed the dark destiny of young Anakin's life.

The *Star Wars* poster I just described illustrates (in a somewhat abstract way) the central point of this chapter. People see and perceive the outside,

> God doesn't call us on the basis of what we are now, but on the basis of what we will become.

but God sees what is within and what we will become.

What we're about to discover in this tenth reference to *'do not fear'* is that God doesn't call us on the basis of what we are now, but on the basis of what we will become. God doesn't see us as we see ourselves or even how other people see us. God sees a bigger person on the inside than what we see on the outside.

In fact, how we see ourselves has got nothing to do with what God calls and chooses us to do. Our purpose in this life is the prerogative of God.

As a Christian, we're not what we were, but we're not what we will be. God is not finished with us. We often only focus on what we *are*, whereas God is working toward what we will *be*.

One of the reasons why so many of us fear doing what God has called and gifted us to do is that we only see our lives for what they were or are. God, however, sees the end from the beginning.

Gideon is a prime biblical example of the fear of being rejected because of how we see ourselves. This chapter's reference to *'do not fear'* is found in Judges 6:23, but we'll cover the story from verses 11–23.

Israel's cycle

Let's establish the historical context before we centre in on this chapter's main character—Gideon. In the previous chapter, we left the Israelites licking their wounds after the defeat of Ai. After exposing and purging Achan from the community, they subsequently defeated Ai and went on to possess the land.

In the unfolding sequence of events in Old Testament history, we have now moved from the time of Conquest to the time of the Judges. After the

death of Joshua, the Israelites deteriorated as a people and descended into an unfortunate cycle of:
- Rebelling against the Lord
- Incurring retribution for their sin
- Eventually coming to repentance
- Being rescued by a deliverer.

The 'Judges' were men and women God raised up to rescue Israel from their oppressors and to lead them in their struggle to become the covenant people of God in the land of promise.

In the immediate context, Israel had just had forty years of peace after Deborah and Barak's decisive victory over Sisera and his forces.

Midianite Oppression

The first 10 verses of Judges 6 set the scene. As always, the cycle of rebellion against God continued. *'Again the Israelites did evil in the eyes of the Lord.'* (Judges 6:1) Their punishment was seven cruel years of oppression at the hands of the Midianites.

This was far worse than just an occupation, because the Israelites couldn't even live in their own homes. They dwelt in mountain clefts, caves and strongholds. Whenever the Israelites planted crops, the Midianites, Amalekites and other Eastern peoples invaded the country. They would spread out and camp *on* the crops to waste and ruin them.

In addition, they ruthlessly slaughtered the livestock of the Israelites, and devastated their ability to subsist. After seven long years of no home, no food, no normality, no peace, no rest, no joy and no hope, but pillaging, ravaging, wasting and impoverishment, the Israelites '...*cried out to the Lord for help.*' (Judges 6:6)

God hears the cry of the oppressed—even when the oppression is brought on by our own choices and actions.

In answer to their cry, God sent an unnamed prophet who essentially brought this message from the Lord: 'You have not listened to me. So, you are wearing the consequences.'

The Lord, however, did not treat them as their sin deserved. The Lord's great care and compassion for his people moved and compelled him to personally help his suffering people. God was about to answer their pleas by raising up an unlikely rescuer and deliverer. What we see is that God hears the cry of the oppressed—even when the oppression is brought on by our own choices and actions.

Gideon

At this point in the story, the Scripture introduces us to Gideon: '*The angel of the Lord came and sat down under the oak in Ophrah that belong to Joash the Abiezrite, where his son Gideon was threshing wheat in a winepress to keep it from the Midianites. When the angel of the Lord appeared to Gideon, he said, "The Lord is with you, mighty warrior."'* (Judges 6:11–12)

The text records that Gideon was '...*threshing wheat in a winepress...*' This was significant. Gideon had evidently devised a covert system of producing food so the Midianites wouldn't come and steal their food. It would have been very difficult to winnow the wheat in a narrow, small, troughlike winepress, rather than a flat and wide threshing floor.

This shows us that despite the privations and dangers, Gideon was industrious. He did not allow his external environment or circumstances to neutralise or atrophy his life. He got on with it.

While he was stealthily winnowing the wheat, '...*the angel of the Lord appeared*' to him. The expression 'angel of the Lord' is another way of saying the Lord himself in an angelic form.

Mighty Warrior? Who me?

'*When the angel of the Lord appeared to Gideon, he said, "The Lord is with you, mighty warrior."*' These words astonished, perplexed and, possibly, dumbfounded Gideon. Given the context of his life, this was a powerful prophetic statement. The prophetic declarations of God unveil his intentions, will and purpose.

Let's repeat the basic lesson of this chapter: God doesn't see us as we see ourselves. God sees a bigger person on the inside, than what we see on the outside. God sees what we will become; we see what we presently are. God doesn't call us on the basis of what we are now, but on the basis of what we will become.

The Lord didn't see a 'nobody' doing 'nothing' of significance. The Lord saw Gideon's prophetic potential. The Lord called him what he would become—a mighty warrior!

You must have the wrong man

Gideon baulked at this statement. Even though the angel's words were directed to him personally, Gideon tried to evade the implication and application: *'But sir, if the Lord is with us, why has all this happened to us? Where are all his wonders that our fathers told us about when they said, "Did not the Lord bring us up out of Egypt?" But now the Lord has abandoned us and put us into the hands of the Midianites.'* (Judges 6:13)

These were perfectly reasonable questions to ask. This was an accurate summation of how things were. Interestingly, the Lord didn't answer his questions, nor explain the 'why'.

The Lord hadn't appeared to bring explanation; the Lord was appearing to bring divine intervention. The solution was Gideon.

'The Lord turned to him and said, "Go in the strength you have and save Israel out of Midian's hand. Am I not sending you?"' (Judges 6:14)

Another phrasing of the Lord's words to Gideon may be, 'Gideon, there is more to you than what you realise. It may be raw and undeveloped, but as I have searched your heart I have seen an inward strength. I see that you have what it takes. Given the right opportunity you will flourish and rise. Your destiny is linked to your people. In case all of that is not persuasive, remember *I* am sending you. I will empower you. I will use you. I will accomplish my purpose through you.'

Gideon's realisation

Gideon now understood the Lord had chosen him to redemptively save Israel. This realisation overwhelmed him. Just like so many other responses to God's call—for example, Moses (Exodus 4:1–18) (which has incredible parallels to this passage), Isaiah (6:5) and Jeremiah (1:6)—Gideon initially recoiled at the Lord's words.

> God chooses and uses the least likely and the most unlikely.

God's call just didn't reconcile with how he saw himself. '*But Lord, how can I save Israel?*' he protested, '*My clan is the weakest in Manasseh, and I am the least in my family.*' In different words: 'Lord, I am a nobody from a nobody family from a nobody group of people. I have no influence, no stature, no rank and no authority.'

In response to Gideon's objections, the Lord answered, '*I will be with you, and you will strike down all the Midianites together.*' (Judges 6:16) This shows us that God chooses and uses the least likely and the most unlikely.

God's sovereign calling to serve him comes despite human disqualifications, limitations, frailties, failures, faults, fears, objections and others' perceptions. God's assurance to Gideon was: 'Despite how you see yourself, despite how you feel about yourself and despite the hard circumstances, I am going to use you to set my people free.'

Confirmation

We would think that Gideon would have got 'it' by this stage, but 'no' he sought still further assurance. Out of more disbelief than unbelief, Gideon asked for a sign to confirm and authenticate God's word to him.

The Lord in his grace gave him some latitude. Gideon prepared an offering and brought it to the Lord. The Lord instructed Gideon to place the meat and unleavened bread on a designated rock. The Lord touched them with the tip of his staff. Then…

'Fire flared from the rock, consuming the meat and the bread. And the angel of the Lord disappeared. When Gideon realised that it was the angel of the Lord, he exclaimed, "Ah, Sovereign Lord! I have seen the angel of the Lord face to face."' (Judges 6:21–22)

Gideon now realised this was not just an ordinary angel, but *the* angel of the Lord. He realised he had seen God and lived. Consistent with many Old Testament characters, he believed that it was impossible and impermissible to see God and live.

In strict context, this is why the Lord answered, *'Peace!* **Do not be afraid.** *You are not going to die.'* (Judges 6:23) Gideon needed reassurance he was not going to die, but, given the broader flow of the passage, I would suggest the *'do not be afraid'* is also God's way of encouraging Gideon not to hold back from doing what he was being called to do. He did not need to fear death, nor did he need to fear doing what God was calling him to do.

> Do not fear even if what he's calling you to do seems bigger than you, remembering the Lord sees a bigger person on the inside than what you see.

Conclusion

In our lives, do not fear doing whatever God is calling you to do.

Do not fear even if what he's calling you to do seems bigger than you, remembering the Lord sees a bigger person on the inside than what you see.

Do not fear believing the prophetic and God-given dreams.

Do not fear being who you are called to be.

Do not fear because you *are* a *mighty warrior*.

Do not fear because God didn't call you on the basis of what you are now but on the basis of what you would become.

11

Fear that What God Has Promised Will Not Come to Pass

1 Samuel 23:15–18

The test of *delay* is one of the most difficult struggles in the Christian experience. The test of delay is the time period between receiving a promise or a clear 'word' from God and the fulfilment. The intervening period can sometimes 'test' our patience, resolve and faith.

As we'll see in this chapter, the delay can sometimes bring complications or contradictions. These often drive us to wrestle with internal questions like:

- 'Did I really hear from God?'
- 'Is it going to happen?'
- '*If* God has spoken, why do the circumstances seem completely the contrary?'
- 'What can I do to make it happen?'

If we don't find satisfactory biblical answers, the result may be fear—fear that what God has promised will not come to pass.

The story we'll focus on in this chapter will also show us that God always has the right person at the right time with the right message to encourage us and fortify our faith to keep waiting. The central lesson of this chapter is not to fear in the delay because God's purposes will not be thwarted by the delay.

Historical background

Our eleventh reference to '*do not fear*' is found in 1 Samuel 23:15–18, particularly verses 16–17.

We have now passed from the time of the Judges to the period called the Monarchy. After the period when the Judges ruled, the people craved a king so they could be like the neighbouring nations.

> There are times in our lives when God will send someone to help us do something we can only do for ourselves— 'find strength in God'.

In effect, they had rejected God as their governing Sovereign, choosing instead to have an earthly monarch. Saul was their first king, but his character flaws soon unravelled his leadership. Through rebellion and disobedience, he was rejected by God.

God chose a new man, David, to be his successor. As Saul recognised this, he tried to kill David to retain his rule and dynasty. For his own safety David became a man on the run.

David was being prepared for the throne, but was in the period between the promise and the fulfilment. He was in the uncomfortable period of preparation and testing. His character, dependence and resilience were being shaped by the delay.

Find strength in God

In this chapter's study passage, David was once again hiding in a stronghold in the desert of Ziph. Saul's son, Jonathan, had come to him. There is a powerful little phrase here that we could almost glance over without really grasping the application. 1 Samuel 23:16 reads, '*And Saul's son Jonathan went to David at Horesh and* **helped him find strength in God.**'

The suggestion here is that David was disheartened. Understandably, life on the run was taking its toll on him emotionally, psychologically and spiritually. Jonathan had come expressly to encourage him. He did so by focusing David on the Lord his God.

There are times in our lives when God will send someone—sometimes a friend, sometimes a preacher, sometimes a book—to help us do something we can only do for ourselves—'*find strength in God.*'

Our text doesn't explicitly tell us *how* Jonathan helped him find strength, but the next verse gives a very big clue: '*Jonathan said, "Do not be afraid. My father Saul will not lay a hand on you. You will be king over Israel, and I will be second to you. Even my father Saul knows this."*' (1 Samuel 23:17)

Jonathan helped him find strength in God by *affirming* the anointing, call and promise of God upon David's life. In essence, Jonathan said, 'David, it may seem that the prevailing circumstances of your life at the moment threaten to kill the word of God in your life. Do not be afraid. Harm will not come. Destruction will not come. Death will not come. God will fulfil what he has said—you *will* be king. I recognise and affirm the anointing and call upon your life. It is going to happen and will come to pass. Do not be afraid—the promise is not dead. Rekindle your faith. Reawaken the promise. Revitalize your expectation. Renew your trust in God. Restore your passion for his Presence. It is just a matter of time.'

When people like Jonathan speak into *our* lives, our spirit is ignited and energised to believe God's promise. We are enabled to endure the 'test of delay' with fresh resolve and resilience.

May each of us be like Jonathan and build others up. Let's speak 'life' into one another. May we affirm God's prophetic promises in other people's lives. There are probably many disheartened people waiting for *us* to help them find strength in God.

Lesson learnt

What happens, though, when there is no-one like Jonathan around to help us? The unfolding narrative shows us.

Sometime later, to avoid Saul's relentless pursuit and the inevitability of capture (1 Samuel 27:1), David and his men, along with their wives and children, went to live among the Philistines. One of their commanders, Achish king of Gath, assigned them the city of Ziglag.

A year or so later, while fulfilling his obligations to join Achish and the Philistine army to fight against Saul and the Israelites, David was reluctantly asked to withdraw from their ranks for fear he would switch sides during battle (1 Samuel 29:1–10).

David and his forces returned to Ziklag to find it had been raided by the Amalekites, and their wives and children had been forcibly abducted (1 Samuel 30:1–3). David and his men were grief stricken and wept inconsolably (v. 4). Picture these tough fighting men broken and doubled up with personal pain. Imagine the sound of hundreds of men howling with grief.

The men's pent up pain turned to anger: *'…the men were talking of stoning [David]; each one was bitter in spirit because of his sons and daughters.'* (1 Samuel 30:6). This was serious: David's life was in danger. His men were bitter toward him. The sentiment toward him was clear: 'If it weren't for *you*, we wouldn't be in this mess?'

He was alone…again! He was personally suffering—*'David was greatly distressed…'* (1 Samuel 30:6) This big brave giant–slayer was crippled by emotional exhaustion, broken–heartedness and distress.

Before we look at how he coped, let's do a very quick recap of his life since he received the anointing to be king:

- Out of raging jealousy, Saul had driven him from his country
(1 Samuel 18:9–29)
- Out of mistrusting fear, the Philistines had asked him to leave their camp
(1 Samuel 29:1–5)

David recognised that what he couldn't find in himself, he could find in his God.

- Out of revenge, the Amalekites had raided his home town
  (1 Samuel 30:1)
- Out of plundering greed, his wives and children had been taken captive by the Amalekites
  (1 Samuel 30:5)
- Out of anguish of heart, his own trusted friends, who he had sheltered, were now threatening to kill him
  (1 Samuel 30:6)

What was David going to do? How was he going to handle this? This time, he did not have Jonathan to encourage him, but 1 Samuel 30:6 explicitly tells us: '...*David found strength in the Lord his God.*' Jonathan may not have been there, but David had learned a lesson from him many years before. David now applied the lesson by finding strength in God for *himself*.

> When we have nobody else to turn to, we can go to our God and find strength in him alone.

David recognised that what he couldn't find in *himself*, he could find in his *God*. He may have lacked courage and strength at that moment, but he drew upon the source of all courage and strength—God himself. David was at the end of his own internal resources, but he drew upon the eternal supply of the life of God.

Perhaps we can identify with David because we, too, may be weary from waiting. Perhaps the stranglehold of fear is tightening its grip on our faith and screaming, 'It will never happen. God's word will never come to pass. Everything is against you. Give up.'

If so, then we need to be like David and develop a capacity to find strength in the Lord for *ourselves*. Each of us must learn to touch God, to break through, to encourage ourselves in him and tap into the unending supply of God's strength.

When we can't hold on to anything else, we can hold on to the character of God. When we have nobody else to turn to, we can go to our God and find strength in him alone. When everything else is uncertain, there are certainties that we can hold on to, such as the…

- Goodness of God
- Faithfulness of God
- Power of God
- Word of God
- Promises of God (in Christ Jesus)
- Spirit of God
- Strength of God

Practical ideas for finding strength in God

Here are three practical ways for how we can find strength in God:

1. Keep a positive (yet realistic) mindset

A first step in finding strength in God is to have the right mental attitude. This means guarding our thought life from being seduced by doubt or discouragement, which are like parasites that feed off our negative thoughts and words.

Instead, take affirmative action by:

- Keeping things in perspective and not allowing things to blow out of proportion in our mind
- Arresting and apprehending any negative thoughts that are inconsistent with God's nature, word and will
- Purposefully and intentionally focusing our thoughts on God
- Affirming and declaring the truth of God's goodness, faithfulness, power and promises
- Adopting an attitude of decisive resolve that says, 'I am going to seek God and reach out to him. I am not going to give up or give in.'

2. Use whatever means we find work best for us to touch God

People reach out to God in many ways. There is not one ideal means or method. It is as individual as the uniqueness of our personality. Here, though, are some ideas:

- Play a worship CD and worship God from your heart until you sense his presence
- Plan a dedicated time of prayer and fasting to seek the Lord
- Withdraw somewhere quiet where you can engage in silent, meditative prayer to wait upon the Lord
- Walk on a beach or in the bush to still your heart and mind
- Attend a prayer meeting or Sunday service where there is life-giving ministry

The goal of all these illustrative methods is to engage with God through prayer until we experience his presence.

3. Pray or seek God until we break through

It's important at times like this to pour out your heart to the Lord in specific, heartfelt prayer (Psalm 62:8; Philippians 4:6–7). Hold nothing back. Freely pour out your feelings. Cry out to God, seek him and call upon his name. It is vital to persevere in prayer and not give up.

One of the central applications of the Parable of the Persistent Widow (Luke 18:1–8) is that God will answer the prayers of his people '*…who cry out to him day and night.*' (Luke 18:7)

Jesus had taught on persistence in prayer once before in Luke 11:1–11. In that passage, it is significant that the disciples, the future leaders of the church, never asked him, 'Lord, teach us to preach.'

Rather, one of them sincerely asked him, '*Teach us to pray!*' In reply, Jesus initially told them the Lord's Prayer (Luke 11:2–4), then the parable of the friend who wanted bread in the night (Luke 11:5–8).

The message of the parable was that even though the 'friend' inside was reluctant and resistant to help, '*…yet because of his* [friend's] *boldness* [in asking] *he will get up and give him as much as he needs.*' (Luke 11: 8) The word 'boldness' can also be translated 'persistence'. Jesus said that the bold and persistent get results in prayer.

In the same flow of thought, Jesus responded to the disciple who had requested to learn how to pray by saying, '*Ask and it will be given you; seek and you will find; knock and the door will be opened to you.*' (Luke 11:9) The principle here is to be persistent. Ask and keep on asking. Seek and keep on seeking. Knock and keep on knocking. Jesus gave the assurance that '…*everyone who asks receives; he who seeks finds; and to him who knocks, the door will be opened.*' (Luke 11:10) The application being that when we are reaching out to God in prayer we must not slacken off or stop, but ask audaciously and tenaciously.

This wasn't the end of Jesus' teaching on prayer. This rich teaching concluded with Jesus contrasting human fathers to our heavenly Father. '*Which of you fathers, if your son asks for a fish, will give him a snake instead? Or if he asks for an egg, will give him a scorpion?*' (Luke 11:11–12) It seems ridiculous and ludicrous that any earthly father would even contemplate such a preposterous response.

Jesus then brought the application, '*If you then, though you are evil, know how to give good gifts to your children, how much more will your father in heaven give the Holy Spirit to those who ask him?*' (Luke 11:13) At the start of the passage, a disciple had asked Jesus to be taught how to pray. Jesus concluded this passage by encouraging him to ask for more of the Holy Spirit, a gift his Father will lavishly give to those who persistently ask.

> When we're filled afresh with the Holy Spirit, we are filled afresh with strength.

Ultimately, if we are to '*find strength in God*', we need the inner strength and power of the Holy Spirit (Ephesians 3:16). From Jesus' teaching on prayer, we've seen that we should ask the Father for more of his Spirit, but keep seeking him until our prayer is answered. When we're filled afresh with the Holy Spirit, we are filled afresh with strength.

Finally

David did find strength in God, but his family and those of his men were still in the Amalekite camp. David *'enquired of the Lord'* to know what to do by asking, *'Shall I pursue this raiding party? Will I overtake them?'* The Lord told David to *'pursue them'* for he would *'certainly overtake them and succeed in the rescue.'* (1 Samuel 30:8)

Despite their weariness, David set out immediately with his soldiers and after a battle which raged nearly 24 hours, he took back everything that had been taken. *'Nothing was missing: young or old, boy or girl, plunder or anything else they had taken. David brought everything back.'* (1 Samuel 30:19) From David's example, after finding strength in God, we should retake what our adversary may have stolen from us.

In this chapter, we have been addressing the fear that what God has promised will not come to pass. This fear normally stems from nothing seeming to happen in the intervening period between the promise and fulfilment. What we've seen is that God will come through *in his time*.

God's purposes will not be thwarted by delay.

In the meantime, though, we can master this fear by learning to encourage *ourselves* in him. We do so through persistent prayer, especially asking for more of the Holy Spirit.

12

Fear that We Will Go Without If We Give to God[13]

1 Kings 17:13–14

A vast majority of Christian people believe the God of the Bible is a miracle-working God. However, there can often be such a disparity between what we say we *believe* and the reality of what we *experience* that we may appear to give only tacit lip service to faith. How can we bridge this 'gulf'? How can we experience miracles in our lives?

A story which outlines a number of principles for experiencing the miraculous in our lives is our twelfth reference to '*do not fear*'. This is found in 1 Kings 17:13–14.

The story centres on a widow with next to nothing receiving miraculous provision through *obedient* giving. Before she experienced the miracle she had to silence the fear that, if she gave to God, she would go without.

Background

Before we examine the specific reference to '*do not fear*', we need to understand the wider narrative. What is the bigger story?

---

13 Some thoughts in this chapter were inspired and adapted from a short but stimulating book entitled '*Living Beyond the Possible*' by Wayne Myers (Evangeline Press: McLean, VA, 2003, pp. 45–47).

As we continue our broad journey through the Old Testament, we've now entered a new phase called the 'Divided Kingdom'. David's dynasty continued to rule through Solomon, then his son, Rehoboam. Tragically, Rehoboam unwisely listened to the advice of his peers rather than the elders who'd served his father (1 Kings 12:1–19).

Consequently ten of the twelve tribes rebelled against him and established their own kingdom called 'Israel' and appointed their own king. The southern kingdom, Judah, was just the tribes of Judah—to which David, Solomon and Rehoboam belonged—and Benjamin.

In the immediate context of our study passage (1 Kings 17), King Ahab was the presiding monarch over the northern kingdom of Israel. He is unflatteringly regarded as a weak–willed, wicked and godless king who cowered to his manipulative wife, Jezebel. Ahab had been leading the nation down a path toward the worship of Baal, a Phoenician deity. This meant there was an incredible spiritual clash between the worship of the Lord (Yahweh) and Baal.

The prophet Elijah had given King Ahab a message from God saying that there would be no rain or even dew in the land until he (Elijah) said otherwise (1 Kings 17:1). Elijah was then commanded to hide by the Kerith Ravine,[14] presumably because Ahab had threatened his life (1 Kings 17:2–3).

After some time, the effect of the drought which he had prophesied began to affect him personally—the brook ran dry (1 Kings 17:7). To avoid hunger and dehydration, God instructed Elijah to go to the town of Zarephath where a widow had been commanded to supply him with food (1 Kings 17:9).

Once Elijah arrived at Zarephath, he saw the lady mentioned in the prophetic word and requested some water from her. As she turned to get some, he also asked for a piece of bread (1 Kings 17:10–11). This brought an immediate reaction. The widow told Elijah that she only had enough food for one last meal for herself and her son, then she expected they

---

14 Kerith was on the east side of the Jordan, not far from Jericho. The term 'brook' probably refers to a river bed with pools of water from the rainy season.

would both starve (1 Kings 17:12). She candidly told him she could not accommodate his request.

Against that backdrop, Elijah gave the unnamed widow very clear instructions for how she was to respond. By unpacking Elijah's words we see a number of principles for how we can position ourselves for the miraculous in our lives.

Subdue the fear that we will go without if we give to God

Elijah's first words to her were, '*Don't be afraid...*' (1 Kings 17:13) The widow understandably feared that if she used the jar of flour and jug of oil for Elijah, she would not have enough for her last meal. This was factually true. One of the basic laws of mathematics is that 1–1 = 0.

Nevertheless Elijah urged her to silence the persuasive and pervasive power of fear by believing that something beyond natural law was possible. He went on to declare that, if she did what God was telling her to do, she would experience a miracle of divine provision until the famine ended (1 Kings 17:14). One definition of a 'miracle' is that it is a suspension or transcendence of natural law.

> If we give in obedience to a specific directive from God, we are positioning our lives for divine intervention.

An illustration of this is how an aeroplane takes off and maintains flight. The law of gravity is a powerful force. Aeroplanes weigh many thousands of tonnes, especially a fully fuelled and loaded Boeing 747 400 or an Airbus A 380. As an aircraft hurtles down a runway, another law comes into play which transcends the law of gravity—the law of aerodynamics. If there is enough velocity caused by propulsion, the aeroplane reaches a certain speed at which the air pressure over the surface of the wing is less than the air pressure flowing under the wing. The result is 'lift'.[15] Gravity can no

---

15 'Lift' relies on the second and third of Newton's laws of motion: The net force on an object is equal to its rate of momentum change and to every action there is an equal and opposite reaction.

longer keep its grasp upon the aeroplane because a new law (aerodynamics) has lifted it into new altitudes. As long as the propulsion is sustained, the aircraft will remain flying.

In the same way that the law of aerodynamics transcends the law of gravity, Elijah assured the widow that her obedience to a specific word from God would propel her out of the jurisdiction and restriction of natural law (1–1 = 0) and bring her under the jurisdiction and dominion of the miraculous. Her obedience would enable her to live beyond the possible. Her obedient giving would be the equivalent of an aircraft's velocity lifting her into a new principle and dimension of living.

Many Christians do not give to God or his work because they, too, fear they will have less. But if we give in obedience to a specific directive from God, we are positioning our lives for divine intervention.

Prioritise God's work over our own needs

Following Elijah's initial words to not fear, he then said, '...*but first make a small cake of bread for me...*' (1 Kings 17:13) Elijah wasn't being presumptuous, selfish or unsympathetic; he was responding to God's word to him at Kerith that a widow in Zarephath had been commanded to take care of his needs. In this context, Elijah specifically asked the widow to put his needs before her own, or, in different words, to put God's work before her own needs.

> We must do what God is telling us to do in precedence over our immediate needs. The principle is to put God first.

This lady was being asked to supply the needs of one of Israel's most prominent and powerful prophets before the needs of her own son. She would be enabling and energising the mouthpiece of God to speak.

Wayne Myers asks a pertinent question in relation to this story: 'Why would God ask a poor, starving widow to take care of someone else's need before her own? The same reason he asks us to tithe to the local church and to give offerings to its initiatives, community outreach, missions' endeavours and one another's needs… because he wants us to experience the kingdom of God advancing in the world through our personal lives.'[16]

We, too, can share in the expansion of the Kingdom through our obedient giving, as we put God and his Kingdom first. Am I suggesting that we should give everything we have away for the Kingdom of God?

Emphatically, no!

That would be irresponsible and negligent of our responsibilities. My point is that we must do what God is telling us to do in precedence over our immediate needs. This may mean having to reprioritise some of our spending habits. The principle is to put God first.

Give from what we already have

Elijah asked the widow to: '…*first make a small cake of bread for me **from what you have**…*' (1 Kings 17:13) She was being asked to give from the little she *already* had.

As a Pastor, I have had numbers of well-meaning people say words to the effect: 'Pastor Bruce, when my investment yields… or when my business is successful… or if I make enough profit on the sale of my property… I want to give something to the church.'

Very, very rarely has the money ever come through. It is easy to give lip service to God about how much we will give when it relates to something that is abstract. Some people even pray or say such words in the hope that God will bless their investment, business or sale. But if we won't give the $50 that is already in our pocket, why would God entrust us with a million? God doesn't ask for what we *don't* have, but he does ask us to give from what we *do* have.

Even when we do give from what we already have, the Lord is not concerned so much about the actual amount, but about the attitude of our hearts. He desires that we give from the heart.

---
[16] Wayne Myers, *Living Beyond the Possible*, p. 46

> God doesn't want our money; he wants our hearts, our lives… our all.

If our giving is not coming from our heart, it shows that we have two objects of affection, or, as Jesus put it, *'two masters.'* (Matthew 6:24) Jesus stated very plainly that no–one can *'…serve two masters. Either he will hate the one and love the other, or he will be devoted to the one and despise the other.'*

Jesus' conclusion was that no–one can *'serve both God and money.'* It is possible to serve God *with* money, but we cannot serve God *and* money (Matthew 6:24).

An example of this from the gospels is the story of the rich young ruler who wanted to follow Jesus (Mark 10:17–31). He is described as devout, dutiful and well–versed in the Old Testament requirements for knowing and loving God. *'Jesus looked at him and loved him. "One thing you lack," he said. "Go, sell everything you have and give it to the poor, and you will have treasure in heaven. Then come, follow me."'* (Mark 10:21)

The next verse records the tragic response: *'At this the man's face fell. He went away sad, because he had great wealth.'* (Mark 10:22) Jesus knew what was in his heart and called him to sacrifice the one thing that would prevent him from following Jesus wholeheartedly. The problem wasn't that this young man had money, but that money had him. He chose to keep his wealth rather than have eternal wealth in heaven.

Jesus was not against the man's wealth per se. He was trying to untangle this young man's heart from the very thing that was more valuable than his wealth—serving Jesus.

God doesn't want our money; he wants our hearts, our lives… our *all*. If he has our heart, he'll have our money as well as our time, service, gifting, reputation, affections and thoughts.

Back in the mid to late 1990s, I was the leader of a large Christian ministry in Victoria. At the end of my tenure, the leadership team I worked with generously bought me a beautiful gold Tissott watch as a token of their appreciation. It was the first expensive watch I had ever owned. I loved it. I loved wearing it. I loved receiving compliments about it.

In June 2011, I visited Kenya for the first time. I was invited to speak at a very large church in Kayole—a suburb of Nairobi, the capital city of Kenya. The worship service was electrifying. I sensed the manifest, tangible presence of God. As I silently stood in preparation to preach, I had this strong and unexpected impression to give my watch away to the senior pastor.

I bristled at the thought and inwardly resisted the voice of the Spirit. I tried to reason with God, but I knew it was his voice and presence. Who can ever argue with God and win? Even while I was preaching I was wrestling with having to give my watch away. I even heard myself say to the congregation, 'You could be one step of obedience away from the greatest breakthrough you have ever seen.' These words resonated in my own heart more so than those of my listeners that morning.

I wish I could say that I yielded to the Spirit's prompting and cheerfully gave my watch to the Pastor immediately. But I have to concede that I didn't give it to him. I rationalised that I needed to speak with my wife first. In my own logic, I reasoned that maybe it was a test like Abraham's willingness to sacrifice Isaac. I flew home with my watch firmly placed on my wrist.

When I got home, I spoke to my wife who told me in no uncertain terms that I should have been obedient to God… immediately. After all, she said, it was *just* a watch. From then on I wanted to give it to this Pastor as soon as possible. I considered posting it to him, but I don't have huge confidence in the African postal service. I had to wait a further six months before I returned to Kenya to finally give it to him.

What God showed me through this unusual experience was that the watch was in my heart. I didn't know how much it was in my heart until he asked me to give it away. Sometimes the Lord will ask us to give because he wants to unmask what is in our hearts. What is within our heart is vitally important to God.

Back in the 1970s, my father was the national evangelist for his denomination. This meant a considerable amount of travel. Unlike today, when flights are affordable and accessible, he had to drive everywhere—sometimes thousands of kilometres. On one particular trip he was ministering in north Queensland for a number of weeks.

After a very successful series of meetings, the local Pastor gave my Dad a $5 note as a ministry gift. $5! This didn't even cover his petrol. My dad drove away grumbling to God about the pathetic amount of money he had received. The Holy Spirit spoke some words to my Dad that deeply impacted him. The Spirit said, 'If you keep money out of your heart, I will keep it in your pocket.'

The lesson from this point is to give from what we already have.

Believe in the principles of Scripture in regard to the grace of giving

Elijah gave this widow a very distinct promise that, if she were obedient, then God would supply her needs: '*For this is what the Lord, the God of Israel says, "The jar of flour will not be used up and the jug of oil will not run dry until the day the Lord gives rain on the land."*' (1 Kings 17:14)

Evidently, the widow took the Lord at his word for she '*…went away and did as Elijah had told her.*' (1 Kings 17:17:15). She must have believed the prophet promise through Elijah.

Similarly, if we are to experience miracles in our lives, we need to embrace and stand on the clear teaching of Scripture on principles like:

- Tithing (Genesis 14:20; 28:20–21; Leviticus 27:30; Malachi 3:10)
- Sowing and reaping (Genesis 8:22; Psalm 126:5; Hosea 10:12)
- Sacrificial giving (Exodus 36:5; Matthew 26:7; Luke 21:4; Acts 4:34; 2 Corinthians 8:3–4)
- Stewardship[17]

Here are just a few examples of verses we can stand upon and believe:

---

[17] Financial 'stewardship' is the faithful, planned and responsible use of money in the following ways: budgeting, reducing debt, regular giving (tithing), living within our means, using discretionary money wisely and investing where possible.

- '*A generous man will prosper; he who refreshes others will himself be refreshed.*' (Proverbs 11:25)
- '*A generous man will himself be blessed, for he shares his food with the poor.*' (Proverbs 22:9)
- '*…whoever sows generously will also reap generously…*' (2 Corinthians 9:6)

Be obedient in giving

The bold widow took a step of radical faith by obeying the word of God (1 Kings 17:15). She discovered that she could trust God's word. As she took care of Elijah's need first—even before her and her son's own hunger—God miraculously provided an unending supply of flour and oil '*…in keeping with the word from the Lord spoken by Elijah.*' (1 Kings 17:16) The key was her obedience.

Supernatural harvest

The widow's story didn't end with the miraculous provision of flour and oil. Her obedience was a catalyst for further miracles in her life.

Sometime later, the widow's son died (1 Kings 17:17). Grief-stricken, she accused Elijah of being the cause of her son's premature death. Unperturbed, Elijah took the dead body upstairs, stretched himself out upon it three times and cried out to God.

'*The Lord heard Elijah's cry, and the boy's life returned to him*' (1 Kings 17:22).

Arguably, if this lady had not done what God had told her to by providing for Elijah's request for water and a cake, he would not have been in her home when her son died. She would not only have been widowed, she would have been without her son.

> As we put God first, he supplies our needs… our giving could be the seed for a miraculous provision and a supernatural harvest.

Because she was obedient, however, the miracle-working power of God present in the prophet Elijah intervened in her circumstances.

The widow then sustained Elijah's life for nearly three years until the word of the Lord came for him to go and confront Ahab again. Elijah then went to Mt Carmel where he confronted the spiritual condition of the people (1 Kings 18:21) and the prophets of Baal (1 Kings 18:25–29). It was after fire fell from heaven upon the water-logged sacrifice that Israel turned back to the Lord (1 Kings 18:39).

In providing for the needs of Elijah, the widow's obedient giving was instrumental in one of the greatest spiritual revivals, renewals and awakenings the nation had ever known.

Finally

The widow of Zarephath was initially fearful of meeting Elijah's request because she was afraid that she would go without. But Elijah instructed her in the principles of the kingdom of God that when we give, we never lose. As we put God first, he supplies our needs. Like this widow, our giving could be the seed for a miraculous provision and a supernatural harvest.

13

Fear of the Invisible Forces of Darkness

2 Kings 6:16

As Christians, we live in the tension between two realities: the natural (visible) reality we see and experience each day and the supernatural (invisible) realities of God and his Kingdom which we cannot see. The following table draws some comparisons between the two:

Natural world	*Supernatural (spiritual) realm*
Flesh	Spirit
Kingdom inaugurated	Kingdom (yet to be) consummated
Now	Not yet
Transitory (temporary)	Eternal (permanent)
Visible	Invisible
Tangible	Intangible
Audible	Inaudible
Knowable	Unknowable
Logical	Paradoxical
Ordinary	Extraordinary
Mortality	Immortality
Facts	Faith

In comparing the *'momentary troubles'* we endure in this life with the *'eternal glory'* of the life to come, Paul wrote some words which, to me, encapsulate the response we must adopt if we are to live between these two realities: *'So we fix our eyes not on what is seen, but on what is unseen. For what is seen is temporary, but what is unseen is eternal.'* (2 Corinthians 4:18)

Sometimes we can be so overwhelmed or overtaken by our visible circumstances (what we do see) that we don't *'fix our eyes… on what is unseen'* (what we can't see). Consequently, we succumb to natural responses and easily become asphyxiated by fear.

The stories we'll observe in this and the subsequent two chapters vividly illustrate how we can be overcome by fear unless we focus on the greater reality of God and his Kingdom.

Historical background

Even though the Israelites were divided into two nations, the Lord raised up prophets to be his voice to the respective kings of Israel and Judah. Against that backdrop, we'll centre this chapter on a story recorded in 2 Kings 6:8–17, especially verse 16. This is where we find a thirteenth reference to *'do not fear'* in Scripture.

Divine intelligence

In the bigger picture, Elijah had been taken up to heaven and Elisha had assumed the prophetic office and mantle (2 Kings 2:11–14). International relations had deteriorated since the previous chapter because the king of Aram was at war with Israel.

The King of Aram, along with his war cabinet, deployed troops in strategic positions presumably as a base to launch offensives against Israel. Every time, however, the Arameans would seek to 'dig in', Elisha would prophetically warn King Jehoram to be on guard in those exact locations. Jehoram would send reconnaissance forces to authenticate Elisha's words which proved to be true time and time again.

So Israel was always alert and defended wherever and whenever Aram determined and prepared to camp.

Because his plans were continually thwarted, the King of Aram was '*enraged*' (2 Kings 6:11). Suspecting that one of his commanders was a traitor, double agent or conspirator, the King of Aram summoned all his officers determined to smoke out the rat. A spokesman for the commanders answered:

> '*"None of us, my lord the king, but Elisha, the prophet who is in Israel, tells the king of Israel the very words you speak in your bedroom." "Go, find out where he is," the king ordered, "so I can send men and capture him." The report came back: "He is in Dothan."*' (2 Kings 6:12–13)

Surrounded

Enough was enough for the King of Aram. To conquer Israel, he was determined to silence the prophet, so he '*...sent horses and chariots and a strong force there. They went by night and surrounded the city.*' (2 Kings 6:14)

The servant's fear

Elisha's servant woke early the next morning to discharge his duties. Imagine the look on his face as he opened the door and saw the vast, imposing army of Aram with horses and chariots surrounding Dothan. Like a frightened child he quickly ran inside to Elisha where he lamented, '*Oh, my lord, what shall we do?*'

Do not fear

Completely unfazed, the prophet answered with confidence and assurance, '*Do not be afraid.*'

Here is a paraphrased version of Elisha's reply: 'I will tell you *why* you do not need to be afraid: because *those who are with us are more than those who are with them.* All you can see is the natural, visible

> Do not be afraid, because the army fighting for us is infinitely more powerful than the one fighting against us. Change your perspective.

> Our attention should never be on the phenomena of God, but the God of the phenomena.

and tangible. Understandably, you have emotionally convulsed at what you can see. Yes, it does appear overwhelming because it is a large force. But there is another dimension, there is another realm, there is an even greater reality. You see an army, horses and chariots, but there is *another* army surrounding us. This army forms an invisible, impenetrable and invincible barrier between us and them. This army is God's angelic force deployed to watch over our lives to protect and deliver us in times of attack, and to carry out God's purposes for his people (Psalm 91:11; 34:7; Hebrews 1:14). So, do not be afraid, because the army fighting *for* us is infinitely more powerful than the one fighting *against* us. Change your perspective.'

Opened eyes

But the servant still could not *see* what Elisha was talking about. What he *could* see blinded him to the greater realities. Similarly, if we only focus on the visible realities, we naturally respond in fear. So Elisha prayed,

> '"O Lord, open his eyes so he may see." Then the Lord opened the servant's eyes, and he looked and saw the hills full of horses and chariots of fire all around Elisha.' (2 Kings 6:17)

What was Elisha actually asking by his prayer: '...*open his* **eyes** *that he may see?*' The servant's eyes were already open—he could 'see' the Aramean army. There was nothing wrong with his natural sight, and he wasn't in need of an optician or an ophthalmologist. What Elisha prayed was that the Lord would unveil the servant's eyes from the limitations of the physical world so he could *see* the invisible realities. 'Lord, let him *really* see.'

When God opened his eyes, the servant '...**looked** *and saw the hills full of horses and chariots of fire.*' When his eyes were opened, his fear evaporated because he *saw* an even greater reality than the physical reality which produced fear. He saw that the forces *with* him and *for* him were infinitely greater than the forces *against* him.

Eyes that 'see'

There are times when we need to have *our* eyes opened. In saying this, I am *not* saying that we should ask God to give us visions of the spiritual world. We actually don't need visions to really 'see'.

Some people get all caught up by ecstatic experiences and miss the reality. Our attention should never be on the phenomena of God, but the God of the phenomena.

According to New Testament teaching, when we yield our lives to Jesus and receive new life by the Spirit of God—our eyes *are* opened. We 'see' Jesus, we 'know' Jesus, we 'experience' Jesus and we enter into personal relationship with the Living God through Jesus. We don't see him with our human sight, yet he is more real to us than anything we can see.

Peter eloquently expressed this thought in his first epistle: *'Though you have not seen him, you love him; and even though you do not see him now, you believe in him and are filled with an inexpressible and glorious joy…'* (1 Peter 1:8)

As we read and study God's Word, we gain greater understanding of his Kingdom and the reality of how things really are and how things should be. He transforms us by the renewing power of his Spirit and the truth of his Word. It is the Scripture illumined to us by the Spirit which opens our eyes. We believe these things by faith. We then live by that faith. The invisible realities become a greater and more permanent reality in our lives.

In a New Testament sense, 'eyes' are a metaphor for the focus of the inward life which has been illumined by the Holy Spirit through the Gospel and Word of God (2 Corinthians 4:18; Hebrews 12:2; Ephesians 1:18).

So, in encouraging us to ask God to open our eyes, I am saying that sometimes, like Elisha's servant, the physical, visible and tangible circumstances of our lives can be so overwhelming that we naturally respond with fear. At those times we need to ask God to open our eyes.

> Angels are immortal. However, angels are not self-existent (as God), but are creations and derive their immortality from God.

This means, in practical terms, to 'see' in Scripture what is really going on. At those critical moments we must hold onto the greater realities. By faith we 'see' and believe that the forces of the Kingdom of God are infinitely superior to the forces of the kingdom of darkness. By faith we 'see' and believe that whatever our prevailing circumstances, there is a mighty God whose all-encompassing presence will sustain and deliver us. By faith we 'see' and believe that we are never alone, we are never abandoned and we are never forsaken. By faith we 'see' and believe that his power will bring us through.

Angelic forces

Elijah told his servant that there was a greater power for them than was against them. There was an angelic contingent surrounding them which was vastly superior to the Aramean army. Before concluding the chapter, in order to help us in our fight against the fear of the unseen powers, let's take a brief look at what the Scripture teaches about the angelic army.

Features and qualities of angels

Angels are created, spiritual beings which carry out God's will. The title 'angel' means 'messenger' or 'agent'. In the following section are some of the features and qualities of angels.

Spirit beings

When the author of Hebrews contrasted the superiority of Jesus to angels, he wrote that they are '...*ministering spirits sent to serve those who inherit salvation?*' (Hebrews 1:14)

Angels are spirit beings. As such, they are unencumbered by physical and material limitations. Although spoken of in Scripture in the masculine gender, angels—as spiritual beings—are gender neutral. Unlike humans, angels do not marry, reproduce or propagate (Luke 20:35–36).

Immortality

Angels are immortal. However, angels are not self–existent (as God), but are creations and derive their immortality from God. As immortal spirit beings, they are not subject to sickness, injury, ageing, frailty, mortality or death (Luke 20:36).

Individuality

Angels have the attributes and qualities of individuality. They are not merely influences or spiritual 'robots', but spiritual creatures with intelligence and will.

The 'archangels' are revealed as having names. A 'name' cannot be attributed to an impersonal entity, but a spiritual 'person'. The archangels mentioned in Scripture are:

- Gabriel (Luke 1:19, 26)
- Michael (Daniel 10:13; Jude 1:9; Revelation 12:7)
- Lucifer (Isaiah 14:12–14; Ezekiel 28:11–17)

Part of their individuality is free will. Conner writes, 'Angels as men, were created with a free will, having the power of choice. The very fact that some angels sinned shows they all had the power of choice and could either choose to do God's will, or to follow Satanic self–will.'[18]

Invisibility

As spirit beings, they are invisible to human sight, although in carrying out God's commands, angels can, at times, assume a human–like form (Genesis 18:2) and perform human deeds (Genesis 18:8; 19:3).

The author of Hebrews urged his readers not to forget '...*to entertain strangers, for by so doing some people have entertained angels without knowing it.*' (Hebrews 13:2)

---

[18] Kevin Conner, *The Foundations of Christian Doctrine* (Acacia Press: Blackburn, Victoria, 1980): 89.

Innumerable

Angels are innumerable. Only God knows their exact number. Various terms are used in Scripture to describe their incalculable company:
- Legions (Matthew 26:53)
- Host (Psalm 103:21; Luke 2:13)
- Army (Joshua 5:15)
- Thousands upon thousands (Daniel 7:10; Hebrews 12:22)

Ministry of angels

If angels are *ministering* spirits sent to *serve* God's children, the question arises of what does God specifically send angels to do? From Scripture, we see a number of ways[19] in which God used angels:

- *To bring a message to a servant of God in a crisis.* The apostle Paul received a message of assurance from an angel on board a boat in the grip of a severe and life–threatening storm (Acts 27:21–24).
- *To announce an important event.* The angel, Gabriel, spoke to the priest Zechariah about the miraculous birth of John who would be the forerunner to Jesus (Luke 1:5–19). Angels spoke to Mary (Luke 1:26–38), Joseph (Matt. 1:20–21) and the shepherds (Luke 2:8–13) about the birth of Jesus.
- *To strengthen a discouraged person for what lies ahead.* An angel gave Elijah food and drink prior to going to Mt Horeb to meet with the Lord (1 Kings 19:1–8). On two occasions Hagar was encouraged by an angelic voice when she was in a desperate condition (Genesis 16:10; 21:17).
- *To protect and preserve from danger.* Daniel was protected in the lion's den by an angel (Daniel 6:22). Shadrach, Meshach and Abednego were preserved in the fiery furnace by the angel of the Lord (Daniel 3:20–28).
- *To rescue in a crisis.* Lot was rescued by angels just prior to the judgment and destruction of Sodom (Genesis 19:1–24). On the

---
[19] For a detailed list of the ministry of angels in Scripture see Conner, *The Foundations of Christian Doctrine,* pp. 93–96

night before he was scheduled to be executed, Peter was miraculously released from jail after an angel woke him, released his chains and led him out (Acts 12:6–10).

- *To position a Spirit–filled and wise man to share the gospel with a person seeking for the truth.* An angel instructed Philip to go to a particular road so he would intersect with the Ethiopian eunuch on his way home after visiting Jerusalem (Acts 8:26–40).

Angelic army

As we bring all these discoveries together, we note that God has created an innumerable and invisible army of immortal spiritual beings—known as angels—whom he uses to carry out his will to guide, rescue, protect, deliver and minister to us. This army is watching over us and is *for* us.

Personal examples of angelic intervention

I've experienced the intervention of angels firsthand. Here are three short stories that illustrate the protection of angels in my life and ministry.

Many years ago, my wife and I, along with a group of close friends, went on a day trip to Wilson's Promontory, the southern–most point of the Australian mainland. Being quite young, we were playing a game where one group would go ahead and hide, then the other group would come and try and find us. I ran ahead as fast as I could along a dirt path. After some time, my friend, Geoff, caught up with me. His face was ashen and looked shaken.

'Did you see the big snake curled up on the path?' he asked.

'No!' I replied.

Geoff continued, 'I came running down the track after you when suddenly two unseen hands physically stopped me in my tracks. I looked down and there in front of me was a huge snake curled up. Your footprints were on either side of the snake! When I looked behind me to see who had stopped me, there was no–one there.'

Now *I* was ashen and shaken. I hadn't even seen the snake and had run right over the top of it. For Geoff, an angel had grabbed hold of him a split second before he would have trodden on the snake and possibly been bitten.

The second story happened back in the 1980s, when I was a dark-haired, long-haired youth pastor. We had some very exciting years in the mid-80s when we began to see numbers of young people saved out of an occult background. One of the young men, Anthony, was very attracted to the church, but for less than spiritual reasons.

He had fallen for one of the young ladies, Heather, and she had fallen for him. Anthony, though, had not really repented of his involvement in the occult and was still dabbling heavily into all types of evil practices. So I spoke with Heather and tried to discourage the relationship until Anthony was more established in his faith. She, unwisely, told Anthony about our conversation. He was furious and was determined to beat me up for interfering in his relationship.

I emerged from the pre-service prayer meeting the following Saturday night. As I was about to walk down the stairs into the auditorium, I saw Anthony bounding up the stairs toward me. He looked angry and aggressive.

'Who do you think you are interfering in our relationship!' he yelled at me. 'I'm going to get you.'

I could tell by the glazed expression in his eyes that there was a demonic presence operating in his life at that moment. As he got close to me, I physically felt like an impenetrable cushion of air between me and Anthony. He was only centimetres away from me when he realised his arms were pinned to his body by an unseen force. He was unable to move any closer to me and was also incapable of moving his arms. An angel was restraining him and formed a barrier between us. He strained to break free from the invisible grip but simply couldn't.

I'll never forget him pointing his finger at me while his arms were still pinned beside his torso and saying, 'Next time, I'm going to get you.' As he backed away he kept saying, 'Next time, I'm going to get you.'

Because of what happened to Anthony he soon came to a place of repentance and left his life in the occult to follow Jesus.

The third incident happened later. Due to the number of people we had coming out of the occult there was the inevitable need for deliverance—casting out of demons. One time we were driving an evil spirit out of a young man. It was taking some time so we decided to have a quick break.

As I walked away, unbeknown to me, the young man who was lying on the floor reached out and grabbed the leg of a solid wooden chair. With demonic strength he hurled the chair toward me. My colleagues were astonished as the chair hurtled toward my back until, just centimetres away, it suddenly changed direction and fell harmlessly to my side. An invisible force, which I believe was an angel, had protected me from certain injury by deflecting the chair off to one side.

> In regard to the reference to 'do not fear', we mustn't fear evil powers: because the angelic forces of the Kingdom of God are infinitely superior to the forces of darkness.

These experiences taught me a lot about angelic protection. Angels are real. Their power is supernatural and their ministry is heaven-sent. They carry out God's will to minister to our lives in many unseen ways.

Finally

The outcome of the Scriptural story was that the Arameans did actually advance to capture Elisha. Elisha prayed that the Lord would strike them blind, which the Lord did.

Elisha then led them into Samaria where he prayed that their eyes would then be reopened. Israel's king, Jehoram, wanted to kill them, but Elisha would not let him. Instead, they exercised hospitality and let them go. Consequently, the Arameans stopped raiding Israel.

In regard to the reference to '*do not fear*', we have learnt that Elisha told his servant not to fear for the same reason we mustn't fear evil powers: because the angelic forces of the Kingdom of God are infinitely superior to the forces of darkness. We need to change our perspective from what we can see to what we cannot see.

14

Fear of Defeat in a Spiritual Battle
2 Chronicles 20:14–17

Nobody likes to lose. I like sport, especially cricket (the game above all games) and AFL (Australian Rules Football). If there's nothing else on television worth watching I will search every station to find some sport, even lawn bowls or netball, if I'm desperate.

However, unlike a lot of my friends, I don't enjoy boxing, kickboxing or the UFC (Ultimate Fighting Championship). I cannot see the sense of getting into a ring with another competitor whose sole intention is to beat the living daylights out of you.

At least in the *Rocky* films, you knew it was make believe. However live streaming of a major bout is serious business and potentially worth millions of dollars. Consequently, no opponent goes into the match planning or wanting to lose. The stakes—both in terms of the fighter's health and finances—are very high. Therefore, the mindset of each competitor must be one of winning.

By way of parallel, no Christian wants to engage in a spiritual battle and be defeated. Each of us wants to prevail. How can we position ourselves for triumph? One of the keys is to adopt a mindset of victory.

The question is: How do we adopt such a mindset? The story we'll examine in this chapter provides some illuminating and practical insights to answer this question.

This fourteenth reference to *'do not fear'* is contained in a prophecy recorded in 2 Chronicles 20:14–17. It is part of a wider narrative disclosed in 2 Chronicles 20.

The tragic scene (2 Chronicles 20:1–13)

An alliance of evil neighbouring peoples, described as a 'vast army', came to make war against Jehoshaphat and the people of Judah.

Under incredible pressure and stress, Jehoshaphat resolved to ask God for his intervention, so he called the whole of Judah to fast and pray. Their prayer was a heartfelt cry of absolute dependence on God for deliverance which was captured by Jehoshaphat's last sentence: *'We do not know what to do, but our eyes are upon you.'* (2 Chronicles 20:12)

The chronicler describes how *'…the men of Judah, with their wives and children and little ones, stood there before the Lord.'* (2 Chronicles 20:13) The men must have been feeling an acute sense of fear knowing they were about to fight a vast army and face certain defeat. Internally, they must have been tortured with the realisation that their wives and children would be slaughtered or taken into captivity.

The women would have been seized by turmoil with the expectation of losing their husbands and sons. Inwardly, they must have been breaking apart with maternal concern for their little ones. Even the children and infants must have intuitively sensed their parents were fearful. This must have been a heartbreaking scene to witness.

There was a palpable fear of defeat before this battle. Sometimes we, too, can fear defeat in the spiritual battles we face, especially when we're facing overwhelming circumstances. But the Lord was about to show Jehoshaphat and Judah why they didn't need to fear.

Prophetic promise of deliverance

Suddenly the whole scene of despair and desperation changed. The '... *Spirit of the Lord came upon Jahaziel...*' (2 Chronicles 20:14) He declared a powerful prophecy from God: '*Listen, King Jehoshaphat and all who live in Judah and Jerusalem! This is what the Lord says to you: "**Do not be afraid** or discouraged because of this vast army...*"'

Then he explicitly told them the reason why the Lord was telling them not to fear: "*...For the battle is not yours but God's.*"

Further on into the prophecy he declared: "*You will not have to fight this battle; stand firm and see the deliverance the Lord will give you... Do not be afraid; do not be discouraged. Go and face them tomorrow, and the Lord will be with you.*" (2 Chronicles 20:15–17)

The battle is not yours, but God's

Why, according to the prophecy, didn't Jehoshaphat or the people need to be afraid? Because the battle was not theirs, it was the Lord's.

This meant they would not be fighting alone with their own strength, skills and swords. Rather, God himself would fight *with* them and *for* them (as we have seen previously in Chapter 4 when the people faced Pharaoh at the Red Sea).

Jahaziel's words ('*the battle is...God's*') are reminiscent of David's defiant words to Goliath in 1 Samuel 17:47: '*All those gathered here will know that it is not by sword or spear that the Lord saves; for the battle is the Lord's, and he will give all of you into our hands.*'

How to respond to the knowledge that the battle is the Lord's

The prophecy, however, didn't end with the words: '*do not be afraid...of the vast army...for the battle is not yours, but God's.*' (2 Chronicles 20:15) It went on to give Jehoshaphat and the people three very clear instructions for how they were to respond. By implication, these words showed the people *how* they could resist the dual power of fear and discouragement.

> We are not alone, God is for us, God is with us, and God is in us.

We'll examine these three specific directives and apply them to our spiritual battles. These three actions initially seem completely contrary, as if one would neutralise the effect of the others. What we'll find, however, is the same theme that has consistently emerged throughout this book: in the fight against fear there is something *we* must do (humanly) and something only God can do (divinely).

1. Advance against the enemy

The first instruction they were given was: '*Tomorrow march down against them.*' (2 Chronicles 20:16) In a similar vein, the prophecy ended with the words, '*Go out and face them tomorrow and the Lord will be with you.*' (v. 17)

The application was clear: the people weren't to hide, retreat, wilt, cower or fear the battle. In response to God's prophetic promise, they were to face their intimidating foe because God was on their side.

We need to remind ourselves of what we've seen in the preceding chapters: We are not alone, God is *for* us, God is *with* us, and God is *in* us. Therefore we should not flee or shy away from our battles. Instead, armed with the assured promise of God's victorious presence, we should *face* our battles.

Then the Lord said, '*You will not have to fight the battle.*' (2 Chronicles 20:17). However this did not mean Jehoshaphat and Judah were to be passive. They had to move *out* as if they were engaging the enemy.

2. Adopt a posture of fortitude

After being told to march *out* against their foe, they were then instructed,

> Even though the battle is the Lord's, he requires us to have a posture and attitude of resolve, resilience and fortitude.

secondly, to '...*take up your positions; stand firm and see the deliverance the Lord will bring...*' (2 Chronicles 20:17) There was something they had to do (i.e. march, take up positions, stand firm, see), and something only God could do (i.e. fight the battle, bring deliverance).

We must adopt and maintain the right posture in the battles we face. Even though the battle is the Lord's, he requires us to have a posture and attitude of resolve, resilience and fortitude.

The prophet's language reminds us of the Apostle Paul's words when referring to the armour of God: '*Put on the full armour of God so that you can take your stand against the devil's schemes...Therefore put on the full armour of God, so that when the day of evil comes, you may be able to stand your ground, and after you have done everything, to stand.*' (Ephesians 6:11, 13)

'*Stand firm and you will see the deliverance the Lord will bring...*' is the very thing Moses told the Israelites at the Red Sea as Pharaoh and his army approached.

Sometimes, the best thing to do is to boldly declare: 'I'm standing firm. I'm standing strong. I'm not going backwards. I'm looking to God for his mighty deliverance. I'm standing!'

3. Choose not to fear

As a third instruction, the Lord repeated his command: '*...Do not be afraid; do not be discouraged.*' (2 Chronicles 20:17)

God required that Jehoshaphat and Judah not yield to natural anxiety or fear. Similarly, we must respond to the reality of God's empowering and protective presence in our lives by not allowing fear to dominate or dictate our lives. We must choose not to be paralysed by fear and discouragement.

The outcome

After receiving this incredible prophetic word and clear instructions about what to do, Jehoshaphat and the people bowed face down and erupted in praise and worship. '*The Levites...stood up and praised the Lord...with very loud voice.*' (2 Chronicles 20:19)

Their fear was transformed into courage, their hopelessness was turned into assured hope, their spirit was revived and their faith renewed.

Unconventional tactic

In consultation, Jehoshaphat then employed an unusual, unconventional military tactic by appointing 'singers' to march out at the head of the army. They had *no* weapons in their hands, because they were armed with something far superior—*words of praise*.

Picture this ancient army marching out with singers in the frontlines declaring the words of Psalm 136:1: '*Give thanks to the Lord, for his love endures forever.*' The people didn't march out as an army going to war to face an enemy, but as an army returning in joyful triumph after a victory.

What was the result of this unusual strategy? '*As they began to sing and praise, the Lord set ambushes against the men of Ammon and Moab and Mount Seir who were invading Judah, and they were defeated.*' (2 Chronicles 20:22)

As they set out from Jerusalem, the destruction began. By the time the army of Judah had arrived on the scene, the alliance had annihilated one other. All Jehoshaphat and his armies found were dead bodies and spoil.

Even though Jehoshaphat and Judah were seemingly outnumbered and overwhelmed, they did not need to fear because they had the promise that the battle was the Lord's. This one promise from God dissipated their fear. As they responded to the promise by doing what they had been told to do ('*go out and face them*'), the Lord did what he alone could do—win the battle in a divine way.

Power of Praise

Many years ago, I preached a sermon on this story entitled '*Song of the Supernatural*'. It was a simple encouragement to people about the power of praise. From this account

> Praise takes our eyes off ourselves and our problems by placing our focus upon the Lord and his greatness.

I drew five principles of praise we can apply in spiritual battles that are bigger than us.

1. Praise, somehow, invisibly activates the Lord to intervene on behalf of an individual or people

The singers and musicians had just left the temple on their way to the Valley of Tekoa to engage in battle and '...*as they began to sing and praise, the* **Lord** *set ambushes...*' (2 Chronicles 20:22) God responded to their praise by intervening on their behalf.

What actually took place in the unseen realm is unknown. The specific nature of the strategies is a mystery. But we do know that their praise activated God to intervene on their behalf.

Paul and Barnabas were in prison—a dark situation. As they prayed and praised (the same combination as Jehoshaphat), a violent earthquake shook the foundations, '...*the prison doors flew open and everybody's chains came loose.*' (Acts 16:26) Prayer and praise resulted in divine intervention to free them from captivity.

2. Praise focuses our attention on God—his works, character and power

The vocabulary of those appointed to praise was, '*Give thanks to the Lord, for his love endures forever.*' (2 Chronicles 20:21) Their praise was focused on God and his everlasting love. Effective praise centres on God's works, character and power often in total contrast to our human inadequacy, weakness and powerlessness. Praise takes our eyes off ourselves and our problems by placing our focus upon the Lord and his greatness.

If ever we are unmotivated to pray, or feeling spiritually flat, the best thing we can do is lift our voice and hands and praise the Lord because...

- The Lord is good
- His love endures forever
- His mercies are new every morning
- His faithfulness is unfathomable
- His power is immeasurable

3. Praise is recognition of complete reliance upon the Lord

Jehoshaphat and his men marched out praising God with unarmed singers leading the way as a recognition of their dependence upon God. It was a choice not to depend on human strength, but totally upon the Lord's mighty power.

4. Praise is an expression of faith

Praise is, in essence, our verbal response to God's self–revelation. God has revealed himself through his works, Word and ultimately through his Son. As we declare who he is and what he has done through words of praise, we are affirming and acknowledging our faith in him.

In Jehoshaphat's case, they praised in response to the revelation of God as their divine warrior (*'For the battle is not yours, but God's.'*) There is no record of the use of swords, spears, shields or bows. Faith was their armour. Before they began the journey to engage the hostile forces, Jehoshaphat had said, *'Have faith in the Lord your God and you will be upheld; have faith in his prophets and you will be successful.'* (2 Chronicles 20:20)

Armed with hearts filled with faith and mouths filled with praise, Jehoshaphat and his army marched out knowing the Lord would bring about a great victory.

5. Praise brings victories over enemies

The result of their faith and praise is recorded in one simple statement: *'And they were defeated.'* (2 Chronicles 20:22) God had done it for them.

When they actually arrived at the battlefield '…*they saw only dead bodies on the ground; no one had escaped.*' (2 Chronicles 20:24)

Praise brings victory. Praise brings breakthrough.

Finally

Jehoshaphat and Judah initially and understandably feared they were going to be slaughtered when confronted by a massive and aggressive alliance of forces. But the Lord raised up a prophet to give the people a promise that he was their Divine Warrior who would fight for them and win the victory.

This revelation and prophetic reassurance dispelled their fear. They then marched out to war in a posture of faith by declaring and singing the praises of God. Consequently, the Lord decimated their enemies and delivered them.

We must draw strength and encouragement from this example in our own spiritual battles. Though our enemy, the devil, is strong, strategic and wicked, we have the Living God whose resurrected son, Jesus Christ, lives within us through the person of the Holy Spirit.

God has given us 'armour' to protect us (Ephesians 6:11–18), 'weapons' to fight with (2 Corinthians 10:3–5), his Spirit to empower us (Ephesians 3:16), his Word as our sword (Ephesians 6:17), and the name of Jesus as our authority (Ephesians 2:9–11). Through the finished work of the cross, we already *have* the victory in Jesus' name.

Our response to this in our battles should be to also adopt a posture of faith, stand *our* ground (Ephesians 6:11, 13–14) and launch our weapons through prayer (Ephesians 6:18) and praise. By doing so, we resist the power of fear.

15

Fear of Being Overwhelmed by What We're Going Through

2 Chronicles 32:6–8

The best way I can describe the experience was a 'waking nightmare'. I'd flown to India to speak at a seminar in January 2014. I was ill before I left and progressively deteriorated. I was hospitalised within a day of arriving in the north–eastern Indian city of Shillong. To my surprise, the doctors diagnosed inflammation and a severe infection in my gallbladder caused by gallstones. They treated the infection so I could fly home to have the operation to remove the gallbladder.

On the journey home four days later, I flew to India's capital, New Delhi, to connect with the flights back to Australia. I was dehydrated, tired and still in a degree of discomfort. I just wanted to get home. When I was about to check in, the airline's personnel dropped a bombshell: the flight had been postponed for 20 hours due to fog at the airport of origin. Given what I'd been through that week, I was absolutely gutted and despondent.

They tried to get me on another flight, but it all fell through at the last minute. After spending nearly 9 hours at the airport, I was escorted to the taxi rank so I could be driven to the hotel where the other passengers were staying. The airline representative explained to the taxi staff where I needed to go. By now, I was so tired and weak that I could barely keep my eyes open. About 15 minutes later the taxi supervisor asked what hotel I was going to. I explained that I didn't know and asked him to contact the airline staff who would know. Eventually the taxi driver began to drive but he, too, didn't seem exactly sure where I was supposed to go.

We pulled up outside a tacky, dirty hotel in a rundown part of Delhi. There was no reservation for me and there were no other passengers here either. It was now obvious that the taxi driver didn't know where to take me. He rang his supervisor. 20 minutes later we went to another hotel but it, too, was the wrong one. By now, I could barely believe what was happening. I was feeling like the situation was getting out of control. We drove back to the airport where the taxi driver stood around with other drivers trying to decide what to do. After a further 15 minutes, I snapped. I got out of the taxi and firmly told my taxi driver just to drive me to Radisson—a comfortable hotel I had stayed at once before.

As we drove, I saw the Holiday Inn and asked him to pull in there, reasoning it would be a lot cheaper. But it was closed for the night. The Ibis was next door but it, too, was closed. I was nearing the end of my emotional reservoir. While driving down a narrow street back to the freeway, I noticed another hotel which appeared to be open on the other side of a barricade. I asked the taxi driver to stop. He asked the security personnel whether it was open. It was. I was so tired, I got out, paid the taxi driver, manoeuvred over the blockade and made my way to the hotel.

It was around 2.30 am when I walked into the hotel lobby. 'I'd like a room,' I asked. 'I'm sorry, sir, we are fully booked,' replied the receptionist. I couldn't believe it. By now, I was distraught. When you're ill, your resilience and endurance are weakened. I had been praying and asking God for help, but he seemed silent and distant. I explained my predicament and health issues to the hotel staff member. He sympathetically made a call and found a room in the hotel next door—their very last unoccupied room.

As I was checking into the hotel I explained to the young man behind the counter about the cancelled flight and what had happened to me. He suddenly lit up and said, 'Sir, the passengers from that airline are all staying here. Mr Hills, we have a reservation for you already—that's why the room is vacant. You won't have to pay anything.'

Out of all the hotels in the airport precinct, I had turned up at the right one, seemingly by accident. Until this point, I had felt overwhelmed by what was happening to me. It felt out of control. As mentioned, it was like a waking nightmare. I suddenly realised that even though I was not conscious of God or his presence, he was working for me. I was in his hands. I did not need to fear.

This chapter will focus on some people who, to a far more intense degree than me, felt a tangible fear that their circumstances threatened to overcome them. We're about to discover that a change in their perspective enabled them to muzzle and master their fear.

Historical circumstances

The story at the centre of this chapter is mentioned three times in Scripture: 2 Chronicles 32:6–8, 2 Kings 18:17–19:37 and Isaiah 36–37. If something is recorded three times in God's Word then it would be prudent to take a good look at the embedded spiritual truth. A fifteenth reason why we are told not to fear in the Old Testament is found in the first of these references: 2 Chronicles 32:6–8.

The king of Assyria, Sennacherib, had already defeated the northern kingdom of Israel. Judah, the southern kingdom, was vulnerable to invasion and devastation. In fact, Sennacherib had already begun laying siege to many of Judah's major cities.

Hezekiah's response

In response, Judah's king, Hezekiah, assembled a large force of men to bunker Jerusalem down for the impending siege (2 Chronicles 32:1–5). Having fortified the city, Hezekiah then turned his attention to fortify the people. The external defences were

> The call to 'be strong and courageous' is a call to adopt an inward posture of steadfastness and fortitude.

repaired and prepared, but now Hezekiah focused on the internal defences of his people's faith and attitude. After appointing military officers to prepare the people for whatever lay ahead, Hezekiah stood and encouraged the people with the words recorded in 2 Chronicles 32:7–8:

> '*Be strong and courageous.* **Do not be afraid** *or discouraged because of the king of Assyria and the vast army with him, for there is a greater power with us than with him. With him is only the arm of flesh, but with us is the Lord our God to help us and to fight our battles.*'

Hezekiah's words had an impact by striking a chord in the hearts of his people. 2 Chronicles 32:8 records that '*the people gained confidence from what Hezekiah*' said. Let's explore why these words were so effective.

As we have seen throughout this book, the call to '*be strong and courageous*' is a call to adopt an inward posture of steadfastness and fortitude. Hezekiah was indirectly encouraging the people not to entertain thoughts of intimidation or capitulation. Nor were they to allow Sennacherib and his forces to deprive them of courage. From the posture of steadfast resolve, Hezekiah commanded them to '*… not be afraid or discouraged because of the king of Assyria and the vast army with him…*'

Greater power

Why were the people encouraged not to fear the king of Assyria? Hezekiah went on to say, '*…for there is a greater power with us than with him.*' (2 Chronicles 32:7) This was the all–important reason *why* the people weren't to be afraid.

Hezekiah was able to instil unshakable confidence because of his belief that the Lord's power *with* them was greater than the military forces with Sennacherib.[20]

Hezekiah then went on to explain exactly what he meant: '*With him is only the arm of flesh, but with us is the Lord our God to help us and to fight our battles.*' (2 Chronicles 32:8) In Hezekiah's estimation, Sennacherib

---

20 This is reminiscent of Elisha's words to his servant in 2 Kings 6:16 (discussed in Chapter 13)

only had the *arm of flesh*; that is: physical strength, military hardware, an equipped army and superior forces.

The people of Jerusalem, however, had the Lord God Almighty who, Hezekiah said, would *help* them and *fight their battles*. Hezekiah drew upon the great tradition of Yahweh as divine Helper[21] and divine Warrior.[22]

Confidence

Sennacherib did indeed have a strong and powerful army. It could have potentially inflicted a heavy and shattering blow on Hezekiah and Jerusalem. The sheer firepower of the Assyrians would have sapped the confidence and hope of the most optimistic fighter. Far from cowering in defeat, the '…*people gained confidence from what Hezekiah…said.*' (2 Chronicles 32:8)

Nothing about their external circumstances had changed. Sennacherib was still menacing and manoeuvring toward them, and Jerusalem was still under siege.

But something *had* changed—the inward attitude of the people. Hezekiah's words had renewed their belief in God's power being greater than the Assyrians. Because they had been reminded that Yahweh was their divine Helper and Warrior, they had an assurance of divine intervention. These 'greater realities' flooded them with confidence.

Vantage Point

Until Hezekiah's words, it seemed the people of Jerusalem viewed the Assyrians from a natural, human vantage point. This produced the inevitable feelings of powerlessness and fear.

God and Satan are not equals. Only God can create; the devil can only copy and corrupt.

---

21   God as Israel's divine Helper is seen in such Scriptures as Psalm 28:7; 40:17; & Isaiah 41:10
22   God as Israel's divine Warrior is seen in such Scriptures as Exodus 14:14; 23:27; 2 Samuel 5:24; & 2 Chronicles 20:29

Hezekiah, however, altered their perception of the enemy by urging them to see Sennacherib and his army from God's vantage point.

Likewise, our perception of the devil and his power (or whatever we're presently facing in our lives) depends on our vantage point—the perspective from which we are looking at him and our situation. As Christians we must not view Satan or trials from a merely human standpoint, but respond to our adversary and adversities from God's point of view which is revealed in Scripture.

By way of example, King Saul and Israel's army saw Goliath from a military perspective and suffered crippling intimidation (1 Samuel 17:4–11). David, however, saw the same Philistine warrior from God's perspective (1 Samuel 17:45–47) and did not fear but ran to meet him in battle (1 Samuel 17:48).

God and Satan are not equals

In applying Hezekiah's words '...*for there is a greater power with us than with him*', we must remember that our God and Satan are not equals. Only God can create; the devil can only copy and corrupt.

Only God has life in and of himself; the devil is a created being and dependent on God for his existence. Only God is omnipresent, omnipotent and omniscient; the devil is finitely limited to one place at one time, has limited power and does not know everything.

God is full of light and truth; the devil is full of darkness and lies—there is no truth in him (John 8:44).

Jesus is the resurrected son of the Living God; Satan is a fallen archangel, a guardian member of the cherubim (Isaiah 14:11–15; Ezekiel 28:11–19). Jesus lives in the power of an endless life; Satan's destiny is eternal destruction (Revelation 12:4–13; 20:2–3, 10; cf. Matthew 25:41). Jesus has been exalted to the highest place (Philippians 2:9); Satan's domain is a place of misery and torment. Jesus has the name which is above every other name (Philippians 2:9); Satan's name (which means *accuser* or *slanderer*) is lower than the most despicable of all creatures.

There is power in Jesus' name over all the power of Satan and his forces. Satan must submit to the absolute authority of Jesus' name. In Jesus' name, demons submit, demonic strongholds are broken and the presence of evil must flee.

Therefore, there *is* a greater power with us.

Lessons

There are some applications from this biblical story that we can apply to our lives.

1. Remember that the Lord is *our* divine Helper and Warrior

First, God was not only Judah's divine Helper and Warrior, but through Jesus he is as *our* divine Helper and Warrior. Our God helps us and fights for us. Therefore, we constantly need to remember that there is a greater power with us than any power that is against us. Whatever circumstance or 'enemy' we face—physical, emotional, financial, relational or spiritual—his power is available to bring us through.

2. Adopt an attitude of courage

Second, when the people of Judah heard Hezekiah's words, their attitude was transformed from one of capitulation and fear to one of courage and determination. Likewise, our response to the Lord being our divine Helper and Warrior should be to adopt an attitude of courage. Our courage is built and based on the victory of the cross, our position 'in Christ' and the authority we have in Jesus' name. Therefore, let us *be* courageous and face whatever we need to face in Jesus' name.

3. Respond in faith and trust

Third, Hezekiah strongly accented the need for the people to respond with an attitude of trust and dependence. Their faith in the revelation of God as divine Helper and Warrior fortified their confidence and filled them with an expectation of divine intervention. Similarly, this should fill us with profound confidence. Confidence should never be mistaken as cockiness or self-assuredness, but a humble dependence and reliance on the Lord.

This thought of dependence on God is captured in Psalm 20:7–8 which says:

> '*Some trust in chariots and some in horses, but we trust in the name of the Lord our God. They are brought to their knees and fall, but we rise up and stand firm.*'

4. Prayer

Sometime later, Sennacherib sent another delegation with the expressed purpose of demolishing the people's new found confidence. He mocked and demeaned the Lord and the people's faith in him. Sennacherib went so far as to write letters 'insulting the Lord' by comparing him to the 'gods' of other conquered nations who had been powerless against him.

> The invisible realities of the Kingdom are more real than the visible and tangible challenges we face.

In response, '*King Hezekiah and the prophet Isaiah…cried out in prayer to heaven about this.*' (2 Chronicles 32:20) Hezekiah's reaction to this further intimidation was to fervently pray for divine assistance. Likewise, whenever we feel fear rising within us because of the circumstances in our lives, we need to pray passionately for God's help.

God heard and answered Hezekiah and Isaiah's prayer, but we'll have to wait until the next chapter to see how the Lord did so.

Finally

What we've learned in this chapter is that we do not need to fear being overwhelmed by our circumstances because there is a greater power on our side than any power against us.

Back in Chapter 13 we noted that Christians are living with two realities: what we *can* see and what we *can't* see. What we've discovered over the last

Chapter Fifteen

three chapters (13–15) is that the invisible realities of the Kingdom are more real than the visible and tangible challenges we face.

We've noted that a key to not succumbing to fear in each of these chapters is to respond to the 'greater reality' with faith and focus.

In Chapter 13, Elisha's servant was instructed to change his *perspective* from the armies against them to the divine armies *for* them.

In Chapter 14, Jehoshaphat was commanded through the prophet Jahaziel to resist fear by remembering God's *promise* of assured victory.

In this chapter, we saw that the key to incapacitating fear in our lives was to believe in God's greater *power* over the power of our enemies.

The following table illustrates our discoveries over the 3 chapters:

Person	*Enemy*	*Why not to fear*
Elisha & his servant	Army of Aram	Greater **perspective**
Jehoshaphat & Judah	Alliance of armies	Greater **promise**
Hezekiah & Jerusalem	Army of Assyria	Greater **power**

16

Fear of Satan's Intimidating Words

2 Kings 18:17–19:37

Some call it 'unsportsmanlike'. Australian players are notorious for it. Those of us who are loyal, patriotic supporters of the Australian cricket team call it 'friendly, good-humoured banter'. With the advent of microphones placed at the base of the stumps, it is now possible to hear it. I am referring to the practice of 'sledging'.

According to Wikipedia, '*sledging* is a term used in cricket to describe the practice whereby some players seek to gain an advantage by insulting or verbally intimidating the opposing player.' [23]

The purpose of 'sledging' is 'to try to weaken the opponent's concentration, thereby causing him to make mistakes or underperform.' [24]

On a far more serious and sinister scale, this is often Satan's tactic with us. He seeks to undermine our focus and faith with his insidious and devious words. If Satan can intimidate, he will dominate. Intimidation breeds fear but domination breeds failure. This chapter will explore how we can neutralise the fear that stems from Satan's intimidating words.

---

23 http://en.wikipedia.org/wiki/Sledging_(cricket), May, 2014
24 ibid

Review

In the last chapter, we mentioned that the story of Hezekiah's siege by Sennacherib, King of Assyria, is recorded three times in Scripture (2 Chronicles 32:1–23; 2 Kings 18:17–19:37; Isaiah 36–37). A sixteenth reference to '*do not fear*' is found in the second of these references in 2 Kings 18:17–19:37.

In the preceding chapter, we left Sennacherib besieging Judah's fortified cities. Meanwhile, King Hezekiah was preparing Jerusalem for the invasion by reinforcing and repairing the city's fortifications and preparing the hearts of his people (2 Chronicles 32:7–8). We looked at the story from the vantage point of Hezekiah's confidence-building words to the people.

Sennacherib's ultimatum

Hezekiah initially tried to settle for peace by paying tribute. At some point Hezekiah rebelled and refused to pay any longer. So, while Sennacherib was laying siege to the nearby town of Lachish, he sent off a high level delegation, which included his field commander and a large force. This delegation went to Jerusalem to deliver Hezekiah and the people of Judah a very clear ultimatum: 'unconditional surrender' or annihilation.

Sennacherib's intimidation

The Assyrian delegation stopped outside the city's walls and called for Hezekiah. Hezekiah sent the palace administrator, secretary and recorder to meet the Assyrians. The Assyrians arrogantly, defiantly and blasphemously declared: '*On what are you basing this confidence of yours? You say you have strategy and military strength—but you speak only empty words. On whom are you depending that you rebel against me?*' (2 Kings 18:19)

Hezekiah's delegation asked the field commander not to speak in Hebrew so the people on the wall wouldn't hear and understand, but this request only fuelled the field commander to more loudly address all the people.

Among other intimidating things, he sought to undermine the people's trust in king Hezekiah and their faith in God by trivialising and mocking the Lord: *"Do not listen to Hezekiah…Make peace with me and come out to me… Choose life and not death! Do not listen to Hezekiah, for he is misleading you when he says, 'The Lord will deliver us…' Has the god of any nation ever delivered his land from the king of Assyria?... Who of all the gods of these countries has been able to save this land from me? How then can the Lord deliver Jerusalem from my hand?"* (2 Kings 18:31–35)

Hezekiah's response and Isaiah's prophecy

When these words were relayed to Hezekiah, he tore his clothes and put on sackcloth (2 Kings 19:1). This was now a very serious situation. It was one thing to have courage and faith with a mere threat (as we saw in the previous chapter), but quite another now that the threat had materialised.

Hezekiah then sent his administrator and some priests to the prophet Isaiah to ask for prayer (2 Kings 19:2–4). In reply, Isaiah said to them, '*Tell your master, "This is what the Lord says: **Do not be afraid** of what you have heard—those words with which the underlings of the king of Assyria have blasphemed me. Listen! I am going to put such a spirit in him that when he hears a certain report, he will return to his own country, and there I will have him cut down with the sword."*' (2 Kings 19:6–7, emphasis mine)

> Intimidating and duplicitous words can produce fear in our minds and hearts unless we are vigilant.

Sennacherib (and Satan's) tactic

Isaiah said something which has great relevance for us in our battle with fear. '*Do not be afraid of what you have heard—those words from the underling of the king of Assyria have blasphemed me.*' (2 Kings 19:6) Isaiah specifically urged Hezekiah not to allow fear to spawn from what he had '*heard*' from Sennacherib's field commander. The implication is that intimidating and duplicitous *words* can produce fear in our minds and hearts unless we are vigilant.

Sennacherib's field commander's specific tactic was to speak insidious *words* in an attempt to undermine Hezekiah's confidence and faith in God. This, too, is Satan's tactic with us.

It is rare that anyone will audibly hear the words of Satan himself (like Jesus in the wilderness). It is more likely that Satan will use the words of others to sow his pervasive and perverted words.

A prime example of this is found in Matthew 16 where Jesus began to explain to his disciples that he was about to suffer and be executed. Verse 22 records how '*Peter took him aside and began to rebuke him, "Never, Lord!" he said. "This shall never happen to you!"*'

Paraphrased, Peter was saying, 'Surely that can't be God's will for you—it doesn't make sense.'

Jesus, however, '*turned and said to Peter, "Get behind me, Satan! You are a stumbling block to me; you do not have in mind the things of God, but the things of men."*' (Matthew 16: 23)

Jesus attributed the source of Peter's words to *Satan*. This is all the more surprising because just moments before Peter had declared one of the most powerful declarations of revelation ever spoken: '*You are the Christ, the Son of the living God.*' (Matthew 16:16) Jesus had acknowledged that the source of Peter's words in that case was not human, but divine ('*my father in heaven*' in 16:17).

As Boice notes, 'One moment Peter is God's mouthpiece. The next moment he is a mouthpiece for the devil.'[25]

When God's purposes ran contrary to Peter's purposes, he unwittingly and unsuspectingly spoke words inspired by Satan to divert and dissuade Jesus from this seemingly senseless course. Likewise, there can sometimes be people in our lives who unwittingly and unsuspectingly speak Satan's mind into our lives.

---

[25] James Montgomery Boice, *The Gospel of Matthew, Volume 1, The King and His Kingdom*, (Grand Rapids, MI: Baker, 2001): 313.

We mustn't let the 'Sennacheribs' or 'Peters' in our lives whisper words that undermine our faith in God or are contrary to God's will. We must be careful not to subtly let Sennacherib seduce us like the serpent did to Eve by seductively appealing to our intellect, *'Did God really say?'* (Genesis 3:1; cf. 2 Corinthians 11:3).

> When our confidence and faith are weakened, the first casualty is our resistance to fear.

There is no suggestion Peter was demon–possessed and required exorcism. In all probability, he simply lacked understanding of Christ's redemptive mission that caused him to interpret Jesus' words on a purely human level. He unknowingly became a channel of Satanic thought.

Maybe, like me, you've heard or thought the follow words:
- What's the point in fighting? Isn't it futile?
- You just haven't got what it takes
- You're not going to make it
- You've been this way for a long time, so why should anything really change?
- Will God really come through?
- Where are the miracles you've heard about? They're just a myth!
- Why should things be any different in the future than they have in the past?
- God hasn't come through before, so why should now be any different?
- You know other people whom God has let down, so why would he help you?
- You've failed so many times before, so why not just surrender?

Unless we are watchful and wary, these words can subtly corrode our confidence in God and his Word. When our confidence and faith are weakened, the first casualty is our resistance to fear. When our resistance erodes, fear begins to germinate in our hearts and minds.

Satan's words will have power and produce fear *if* we let them. If, however, we listen and respond to the Lord's words, Satan's words will not have the power to produce fear.

Why Hezekiah didn't need to fear

In his prophecy, Isaiah gave Hezekiah *the* reason why he did not need to fear. 2 Kings 19:7 continues: '*...Listen! I am going to put such a spirit in him that when he hears a certain report, he will return to his own country, and there I will have him cut down with the sword.*'

In essence, Isaiah told Hezekiah not to fear because the intimidating words of Sennacherib's underling would be invalidated and superseded by God's words. The field commander expressed the will of his master (Sennacherib), but Isaiah prophesied the will of his Master (the Lord). Sennacherib's plans and purposes did not conform to God's, so they would be quashed and overruled. The *Lord's* will would be done, not the King of Assyria's.

If we recognise fear taking root as a result of Satan's poisonous words, we need to apply this Scripture: '*Do not be afraid of what you have heard...*'

We do not need to fear because Satan's will and words, like Sennacherib's, are invalidated and superseded by God's will and words.

Whenever we feel intimidated, besieged or dominated, may we not listen to Satan's contorted words because our God can silence our enemy, break his siege and deliver us.

Some practical lessons

A practical lesson, in this context, is to be careful who we listen to. Sennacherib used his emissary—the field commander—to declare his words to Hezekiah. As we have seen, Satan will often use people, sometimes those close to us, to inject his subversive and undermining words. In some circumstances, we may not be able to deafen our ears to what someone is audibly saying, but we can take decisive action so that those words do not inaudibly affect or infect us.

It almost goes without saying, but Jesus did not let Satan or Peter get away with their words. In the wilderness, Jesus responded to Satan's temptation by declaring, '*Away from me, Satan.*' (Matthew 4:10) To Peter, he responded to his Satan–inspired reaction in a similar way by saying, '*Get behind me, Satan!*' (Matthew 16:23)

Therefore another practical key to silence and subdue words which have a satanic source is to verbally reject them by commanding him to be silent and flee in Jesus' name. In addition, we should declare words that affirm our faith in God. By doing so, we are simultaneously expressing our belief in God's word while repudiating Satan's words.

The finale to the story

Events transpired exactly as Isaiah had prophesied. Reports came to the field commander and Sennacherib himself of potential threats. As they withdrew to deal with these, they sent one insulting last message to Hezekiah seeking to undermine his faith (2 Kings 19:9–13).

Hezekiah's response was to take the letter into the Lord's temple and passionately pray for divine intervention. God heard the prayer and answered with a prophetic promise through Isaiah of deliverance (2 Kings 19:20–34, specifically vv. 32–34).

The result was immediate and decisive. '*That night the angel of the Lord went out and put to death a hundred and eighty-five thousand men in the Assyrian camp… So Sennacherib…broke camp and withdrew.*' (2 Kings 19:35–36) After his humiliating return to Nineveh, Sennacherib was executed by two of his own sons (2 Kings 19:37).

The Lord fought for Hezekiah and the people of Jerusalem. God then gave the people peace and rest along all their borders. Hezekiah became highly esteemed by the neighbouring peoples (2 Chronicles 32:22–23).

The principle that undergirds this entire chapter is that we do not need to be afraid of the intimidating words and will of our enemy because they are neutralised by the words and will of our God. The principal lesson is to be very careful and selective to whom we listen, and discerning in how we respond to the words we detect have come from our adversary.

17

Fear that God Has Rejected or Forsaken Us

Isaiah 43:1–7

Over the years, I've read a number of surveys to ascertain what people most fear. Collating the data, here are the top ten responses. Some are very surprising. We'll countdown from the tenth worst fear to people's worst fear.

10. Flying
9. Venomous creatures (such as spiders and snakes)
8. Closed spaces (claustrophobia)
7. Heights
6. Ghosts (paranormal)
5. Dark
4. Rejection
3. Loneliness
2. Death
1. Public speaking

What intrigued me the most was that the major fears weren't the *external* dangers (such as dogs, ghosts or claustrophobia), but things which may cause *internal* danger (such as rejection, loneliness or embarrassment).

The fear of being rejected and alone is very real. This is the position the people of Judah found themselves in our seventeenth reference to 'do not fear' in the Old Testament.

Historical background

In our journey through the Old Testament, we have now moved from the period known as the Divided Kingdom to the Exile. Sadly, despite the many deliverances the Lord wrought for his people, they still constantly rebelled and refused to listen to his prophets. Inevitably, as an act of judgment, the people were forcibly deported and exiled to Babylon.

However, over 100 years *before* the exile, the prophet Isaiah 'saw' this and wrote down prophecies full of comfort and promises of restoration. These are recorded in what we know as Isaiah chapters 40–66. Even though the Lord knew the people would forsake him, he nevertheless promised *in advance* to redeem them.

Judah's feelings of abandonment

We find a greater concentration of references to '*do not fear*' in Isaiah than in any other place in Scripture (35:4; 41:10,13–14; 43:1,5; 44:2, 8; 54:4).

These references portray a people who were crippled by one great fear: that God had forsaken, abandoned or rejected them. Their state of mind even caused them to wonder whether he had ever been theirs in the first place. This fear literally drained them of hope for the future.

In response, the Lord addressed that very fear by speaking words of assurance and consolation. We'll now examine a number of the references to '*do not fear*' in Isaiah to ascertain *why* God specifically told them that they did not need to fear being forsaken.

Created and chosen to be the people of God

In a number of passages in Isaiah where references to '*do not fear*' are found, the Lord revealed himself as the One who brought them into existence as his people. He '*created*' and '*formed*' them to be '*his*' exclusive people through the Patriarch Jacob (Isaiah 43:1). This people whom he had '*made*', '*formed in the womb*' (Isaiah 44:2), and '*called*' ('summoned'

Isaiah 44:1) from the '*ends of the earth*' (Isaiah 41:9), had been specifically '*chosen*' to be God's '*servant*', God's '*people*'.

The Lord said in reassuringly explicit language, '*I have chosen you and not rejected you*' (Isaiah 41:9) before adding, '*So do not fear...*' (Isaiah 41:10). In essence, God said, 'I have never abandoned, orphaned, forsaken or forgotten you. You have always been, and will never cease to be, my people. I am yours and "*...you are mine.*"' (Isaiah 43:1)

In other places in the Old Testament, the Lord called them '*his own*' people (1 Samuel 12:22; Psalm 100:3), '*a people holy to the Lord*' (Deuteronomy 7:6), '*chosen*' to be '*his treasured possession*' (Deuteronomy 14:2; Exodus 19:5), exalted above the nations (Deuteronomy 26:19), who he '*blesses... with peace*' (Psalm 29:11) and guides '*like a flock*' (Psalm 78:52).

Putting all these references together, we see that a first reason why the people did not need to fear God's rejection was that God had made them his own people by his providence and purpose. They belonged to him. As such, he could never forsake them. Far from rejecting his people, the Lord promised his: continual presence ('*I am with you*'); fortifying strength ('*strengthen you*'); divine help[26] ('*help you*') and sustaining power ('*uphold you*') (Isaiah 41:10).

By way of parallel, we do not need to fear abandonment by God because as believers in Jesus Christ as Lord and Saviour, we are created and chosen to be God's people. We have been:

- Redeemed to be God's people by the sacrifice of Jesus' blood (Ephesians 1:7; 1 Peter 1:18–19)
- Adopted into God's family (Romans 8:15)[27]
- Indwelled by the Spirit (Romans 8:9; 1 Corinthians 3:16) by whom we can address God as our '*Abba, Father.*' (Romans 8:15)
- Assured of our salvation by the Holy Spirit who 'witnesses' (testifies) '*with our spirit that we are God's children.*' (Romans 8:16)

---

26   Also see Isaiah 41:13–14 ('*do not fear; I will help you*'); cf. Isaiah 44:2
27   Paul's metaphor of adoption is fully developed in Romans 8:12–17. Also see David Williams, *Paul's Metaphors* (Peabody, Mass: Hendrickson): 64–66.

- Endowed with the full rights of 'sonship', including an inheritance as '*heirs of God and co–heirs with Christ.*' (Romans 8:17)
- Sealed with the '*deposit*' of the Holy Spirit who is the '*guarantee*' of our resurrection, eternal life and future inheritance (2 Corinthians 1:22; 5:5; Ephesians 1:14)
- Baptised into the body of Christ (1 Corinthians 12:13), so that we are now '*in Christ*' (Romans 8:1; 2 Corinthians 5:17) and Christ is in us (Galatians 2:20; Colossians 1:27)

We need not fear rejection because we are a '*…chosen people, a holy nation, a people belonging to God…*' (1 Peter 2:9; cf. Titus 2:14)

The Lord's presence with them

Another reason why the people did not need to fear being forsaken was that the Lord promised his constant, enveloping and protective presence *with* them. Consequently, they would never face their adversities alone or in their own strength. With God's encompassing presence, they wouldn't be vulnerable to human threats or elemental dangers, therefore they need not fear.

Immediately after saying, '*Fear not*' (Isaiah 43:1), and reassuring the people that they were, in fact, *his* ('*you are mine*'), the Lord added that his presence would preserve and protect them through future trials:

'*When you pass through the waters, **I will be with you**; and when you pass through the rivers, they will not sweep over you. When you walk through the fire, you will not be burned; the flames will not set you ablaze.*' (Isaiah 43:2, emphasis mine)

> We are not promised immunity from adversity… we are promised God's unceasing, empowering and comforting presence while we pass through them.

They would have a lot more trials to face (*'fires'* and deep *'waters'*) before being restored to their homeland. The words of this prophecy are certainly not a promise of a 'quick fix or a trouble–free future, but of God's sustaining presence right through to journey's end, come what may.'[28]

Likewise, we must not misinterpret the 'fires' and 'deep waters' in our lives as God forsaking us. We are not promised immunity from adversity (remembering James 1:2–4, 12; 1 Peter 1:6–7), but we are promised God's unceasing, empowering and comforting presence (by his Spirit) while we pass through them. Therefore we need not fear abandonment; he is with us (Hebrews 13:5–6; Deuteronomy 31:6).

Redeemed (ransomed)

A third reason why the Lord told them not to fear his rejection was that they would be *'ransomed'* (Isaiah 43:3–4). The general meaning of the metaphor of 'redemption' is that of the payment of a ransom in exchange for the liberation of a person or people. God had determined to redeem his people from exile. It's improbable that the specific nations of Egypt, Cush or Seba (Isaiah 43:3) would literally be substituted for their release or that they would incur the punishment Judah deserved.

To me, the more important emphasis of this metaphor was, in the words of Oswalt, that: 'For God no price is too high to pay for the redemption of his own. He would go to any length to find a substitute for them.'[29] This foreshadowed Jesus who would give *'…give his life as a ransom for many'* (Matthew 20:28). He who *'had no sin'* became *'sin for us'* (2 Corinthians 5:21).

In Isaiah 43:3–4, the Lord revealed why he was willing to *'ransom'* and *'give men in exchange'* for them. In verse 3, '…it was because he was their God, he belonged to them…' (*'For I am the Lord, your God, the Holy One of Israel, your Saviour…'*)

---

28 Barry Webb, *The Message of Isaiah*, The Bible Speaks Today (Leicester, England: IVP, 1997): 175.
29 John N. Oswalt, *The Book of Isaiah Chapters 40–66*, The New International Commentary of the Old Testament (Grand Rapids, MI: Eerdmans, 1986): 140.

However, in verse 4 '…it is because of what they are to him. In neither case is the ransom due to an intrinsic worth in the one being ransomed, but because of who God is and what he sees in them'[30] (*'Since you are precious and honoured in my sight, and because I love you'*). He would redeem his people because of his love, mercy and grace.

By way of application, the notion of redemption (ransom) features prominently in the New Testament in regard to Jesus and his death on the cross. The blood of Jesus was the ransom price by which our freedom was bought (Ephesians 1:7). Through Jesus' blood, we are '… *justified freely by his grace.*' (Romans 3:24–25) His innocent blood was given in exchange for our sinful, guilty blood. His once–for–all sacrifice paid the debt we could never pay. This redemption came 'at no cost to the redeemed; it is a "gift"…Christ's death (for that is the meaning of "blood") was accepted in the place of us "slaves", that we might be free.'[31] Therefore, we do not need to fear God's rejection because we are redeemed.

Past sins and failures will be expunged

A fourth reason given why the people did not need to fear being forsaken by God was that their past sins and failures would be forgiven *and* forgotten. In Isaiah 54, the Lord said:

'Do not be afraid; you will not suffer shame. Do not fear disgrace; you will not be humiliated. You will forget the shame of your youth and remember no more the reproach of your widowhood… For a brief moment I abandoned you, but with deep compassion I will bring you back. In a surge of anger I hid my face from you for a moment, but with everlasting kindness I will have compassion on you.' (Isaiah 54:4–8)

Some commentators argue that *'youth'* refers to the Israelites' time in Egyptian slavery and *'widowhood'*

> We need not fear being orphaned by God because of our past or present sins and failures.

---
30 ibid, p. 140
31 Williams, *Paul's Metaphors*, p. 123.

as the Babylonian exile.[32] Others find the meaning in the context of the shame and humiliation of their childlessness (Isaiah 54:1),[33] their inability to bear fruit for God.

Either way, the Lord declared to his barren and defeated people that the days of shame were over. The record would be expunged. They would no longer live with the constant condemning memory of their past sins and failures. Their *'husband'*— their Maker , the Lord Almighty— and their *'redeemer'*, the Holy One of Israel, did indeed briefly abandon them out of his wounded, grieving heart.

> Once our sins are forgiven, they cannot be used against us again. We're free from their power and penalty.

But now things would be different. In comparison to the brief *'moment'* of *'rejection'* when he angrily *'hid his face'*, the Lord's *'deep compassion'* and *'everlasting kindness'* would bring the people back to full restoration of relationship (Isaiah 54:5–8).

Judah need not fear rejection because the Lord was about to wipe out the record of their past iniquities.

Paralleling this to our lives, we need not fear being orphaned by God because of our past or present sins and failures. As Romans 8:1 declares: '… *there is now no condemnation for those who are in Christ Jesus'*. Furthermore, *'the old has gone, the new has come!'* (2 Corinthians. 5:17), and if '…*we confess our sins, he is faithful and just and will forgive us our sins and purify us from all unrighteousness'* (1 John 1:9).

---

32   Oswalt, *Isaiah 40–66*, p. 418.
33   In the ancient world, childlessness was seen as shameful, the result of some sin or being judged unworthy of bearing a child. A childless woman was considered a failure and suffered humiliation (ibid, p. 418).

Through Jesus' finished work on the cross, we have been pardoned, exonerated, imputed with righteousness, justified, forgiven and delivered from the kingdom of darkness.

David once proclaimed that the Lord '*...does not treat us as our sins deserve or repay us according to our iniquities*', and '*...as far is the east is from the west, so far has he removed our transgressions from us.*' (Psalm 103:10–12)

Once our sins are forgiven, they cannot be used against us again. They are gone. The Devil may remind us of them, but we must not allow ourselves to be condemned. We're free from their power and penalty. There may be a few consequences we still have to work through—which we can by the power of the Spirit—but they no longer have a hold upon us. We are not condemned by our past, but are filled with hope for the future in Christ Jesus. Our past is what the word itself means: our *past*.

Parallel

Paralleling Judah's fragile mindset (outlined on the previous pages), let's identify some similar thoughts we may possibly struggle with:

- Some people question whether God really loves them
- Others believe they have gone beyond the reach of God's forgiveness and grace because of sins they have committed
- Still others feel unloved and unlovable, unworthy and worthless
- Others feel forsaken, abandoned and alone
- Some honest people feel like constant failures and wonder whether it is all really worth it.

Paraphrase of Isaiah 43:1–7

To address these thoughts and feelings, I now offer a personal paraphrase of Isaiah 43:1–7 in New Testament language based on Jesus' work on the cross.

Dear reader, can I encourage you to read the following section slowly, thoughtfully and meditatively. If practical, maybe even read it aloud to yourself to amplify its applicability.

'But now, this is what I, the Lord, would say to you. I am the God who created you. I made you for me. I made you for a divine purpose. I prescribed everything about you to accomplish my will. I am the God who gave you life. But your sin and sinfulness severed my desire for relationship and ruptured my purpose. Because of your sin, pride and selfishness, you once deserved darkness, damnation and judgment.

But now you do not need to fear punishment for sin. Because I love you so much I sent my Son to show you what I was really like. The purpose of his life was death, a vicarious death. He came to take away your sins and the sins of the world. Through his shed blood I have paid the price for your guilty blood. Through his sacrifice, he has become the substitute for your punishment. I have redeemed you, cleansed you, justified you, purified you, exonerated you, fully and freely pardoned you, liberated you and set you free.

There are no words to describe the measure of my love for you, so I demonstrated it through the Word himself—my Son—to show you the depth, length, breadth and height of my love. My love has no extremities, no limits and no escape.

I have called you by name. I have chosen you. I know everything about you. I adore everything about you. You are now mine. Nothing now separates you from my love. I have given you my Spirit to put my seal of ownership upon your life. He will live in you to guarantee that I will raise you from the dead to live with me eternally. By my Spirit you will always have my continual Presence.

Satan no longer has any claim in or over your life. You are now part of my family. I am your Father. You are my child.

This life is full of challenges, tests and trials. I can assure you that I will be with you through every one of them. There is nothing you have encountered, are experiencing or will walk through that I will not give you the strength and capacity to endure. I can redeem any and every circumstance and turn it for good. I am at work in you to shape your character to become more like my Son. I am at work in you to mature you so you can reflect my glory. Some circumstances crush some people, but they will only make you stronger.

You are precious to me. You are more valuable to me than any earthly jewel, gold or silver. I will never exchange my love for you for anything. You are constantly at the centre of my thoughts. You are honoured in my sight. I feel such immense pleasure and pride when I look at you. I will restore you, rebuild you, heal your brokenness and pour my oil on your pain.

All of this will bring me glory. I long for the day when the veil shall be taken away and you shall see and know me as I am. So *stop* fearing abandonment, punishment and judgment. I am, and will always be, with you. Fear not.'

Conclusion

The overwhelming theme of the references to '*do not fear*' in Isaiah is that the people did not need to fear because, despite their failures, they were still the people of God, the Lord was *with* them, he would redeem them and their past sins and failures would never be held against them again.

What does all this mean for us today?

There are times when we as Christians fail and fall just like the people of Judah. There is not a perfect Christian who is reading this book, including the author. Our failures can pervasively infect our thought processes and cause our feelings to descend into a dark place where we fear that God has given up on us. As a Christian, we need not ever fear God's rejection. We are his and he is ours. Because of God's acceptance of us in Christ Jesus, we need not fear being forsaken or abandoned.

18

Fear that Our Message or Ministry Will Be Rejected
Ezekiel 2:6–7

The fear of rejection is a crippling fear! No one welcomes or likes rejection. The pain caused by rejection can affect people very deeply. When we experience the pain of rejection, we often take steps to prevent ourselves from ever being in a position where we could be rejected again.

This reminds me of a small native mammal we have in Australia called an echidna, also known as a spiny anteater. As the name suggests, it feeds off ants and termites. Because it is covered with coarse hair and spines, an echidna superficially resembles a hedgehog or a porcupine. When an echidna is threatened, it curls up into a little ball so that all a predator can see or touch are its sharp spikes. These form an impenetrable barrier to threats.

Echidnas are a great illustration of people who've been rejected. Like echidnas, some people wrap themselves up in a little 'ball' to ensure no one and nothing ever hurts them again. They withdraw from involvement in church to ensure they are never vulnerable again. Tragically, some even give up their ministry and calling.

In this chapter, we'll explore the story of Ezekiel and how the fear of rejection nearly derailed this great prophet from being God's voice to his people. We'll specifically examine what the Lord told him was the key to overcoming the fear of people's rejection.

Historical setting

The book of Ezekiel is set in the period of the Exile. Here's a very quick history lesson to put his prophesies into their context.

Nebuchadnezzar first attacked Jerusalem in 605 BC, which is when Daniel was taken captive. But Judah's king, Jehoiakim, rebelled against Babylon. Consequently Nebuchadnezzar launched a second attack in March 597 BC.

Just three months before the invasion King Jehoiakim died and his son Jehoiachin succeeded him. Nebuchadnezzar took Jerusalem with comparative ease. Jehoiachin along with the queen mother, his wives, servants and 10,000 leading citizens were forcibly taken captive back to Babylon.

Ezekiel's calling to be a prophet

Ezekiel was one of those taken captive when he was aged 25. By birth, Ezekiel was a priest. But in the fifth year of captivity, now aged 30, God called and commissioned him as a prophet to the Jewish exiles in Babylon during the last days of Judah's decline, downfall and final deportation which eventually came in 586 BC.

As part of his calling, God gave Ezekiel an overwhelming vision of his divine glory, reminiscent of Moses (Exodus 3:1–10), Isaiah (Isaiah 6:1–10), Daniel (Daniel 10:5–14) and John (Revelation 1:12–19).

The Lord pointedly said, '*I am sending you to the Israelites, to a rebellious nation.*' (Ezekiel 2:3) To me, God's message to Ezekiel was, 'I am sending you to my people, but they are not listening to me, not responding to me, not obeying me, and not living by my law. They have rejected, abandoned and forsaken me. I am calling you to speak to them for me.'

Chapter Eighteen

Do not be afraid

In this context, we find an eighteenth reference to '*do not be afraid*'. It is recorded as part of Ezekiel's prophetic commission: '*And you, son of man, do not be afraid of them or their words.* **Do not be afraid***, though briers and thorns are all around you and you live among scorpions.* **Do not be afraid** *of what they say or terrified by them, though they are a rebellious house. You must speak my words to them, whether they listen or fail to listen, for they are rebellious.*' (Ezekiel 2:6–7, emphasis mine)

Let me paraphrase the essence of the Lord's words to Ezekiel as part of the broader instructions he was given (Ezekiel 2:3–8): 'Ezekiel, do not let fear hold you back from saying what I tell you to say. Don't fear if they harden their rebellious hearts and refuse to listen. Don't fear even if they scornfully reject or repudiate your words. Don't fear even though they threaten and intimidate your life. Don't fear despite their ears being defiantly closed. This is what I want you to do: just speak what I tell you to speak. Do not fear.'

There is a strong suggestion that, after receiving the call a second time, he resisted and wordlessly protested against his prophetic mission (Ezekiel 3:4–11).

He wrote that '*…I went in bitterness and in anger of my spirit, with the strong hand of the Lord upon me.*' (Ezekiel 3:14) Given the spiritual condition of the people to whom he was called to prophesy, it is understandable why he was afraid.

The central point

Ezekiel was, however, commanded not to allow the fear of rejection to divert or dissuade him from persevering in his prophetic ministry. One of the reasons why God told Ezekiel not to be afraid was that he was going to make him as forceful and uncompromising as his hearers

> Whenever we are rejected, we must always remember that the Lord himself has been rejected.

were stubborn and immovable (Ezekiel 3:8–9). God would fortify him to be as *'unyielding and hardened'* (Ezekiel 3:8) as the people to whom he was prophesying.

In Blenkinsopp's words, 'Ezekiel's determination to speak must be stronger than Israel's refusal to listen.'[34]

The central message of this chapter is that if we have a message or ministry from God and we or our ministry is rejected, we must not allow the fear of further rejection to prevent us from continuing to do what we're called to do. God can give us the internal strength we need to deliver the message, be his messenger or continue in our ministry.

It is tragic that so many Christians are disengaged from Christian service because of fear that the pain of past rejections may recur again.

Whenever we are rejected, we must always remember that the Lord himself has been rejected. The people of Israel rejected the Lord as their King. In some of the most heart-breaking words in the Old Testament, the Lord responded to Israel's demand for a king by telling Samuel, '…*it is not you they have rejected, but they have rejected me as their king.*' (1 Samuel 8:7)[35]

Jesus, too, was rejected. Isaiah prophetically described Jesus as being '…*despised and rejected by men*…' (Isaiah 53:3)[36]

The Lord does *not* want us to be immobilised by the fear of rejection. On the contrary, he understands and can strengthen us—as he did Ezekiel—to rise up and serve him wholeheartedly, obediently and, by implication, fearlessly.

Three reasons why Ezekiel should not fear rejection

There are three things interwoven in Ezekiel's prophetic commissioning (Ezekiel 2:8 –3:3; 3:8–11) that reveal *why* Ezekiel did not need to fear rejection in bringing God's word to the exiled people.[37]

---

34 Quoted in Christopher J. H. Wright, *The Message of Ezekiel*, Bible Speaks Today (Leicester, UK: IVP, 2001): 59.
35 For other references to God being rejected see Psalm 81:11; Proverbs 1:24; Luke 7:30.
36 For examples of Jesus being rejected see Matthew 8:34; Mark 6:3; Luke 4:28–29; 23:18; John 1:11; John 12:48.
37 Wright, *The Message of* Ezekiel, pp. 57–62.

First, **Ezekiel was being sent by the Holy Spirit**. As Wright notes, 'The role of the Spirit of Yahweh in the ministry of Ezekiel is one of the main distinctives of his book.'[38]

The Spirit 'came into' him, 'raised' him to his feet and opened Ezekiel's ears to hear his voice (Ezekiel 2:2). In the next two verses, the first words Ezekiel heard the Holy Spirit say were: '*I am sending you…*'

Ezekiel was not going on his own initiative, nor was he being sent as a delegate by other people. Significantly, Ezekiel was sent by the Holy Spirit. This was important for Ezekiel because he was being sent to prophesy to his own people—the exiled Israelites. The Spirit warned him that they were '*rebellious*' (Ezekiel 2:3, 5–8), '*obstinate and stubborn*' (Ezekiel 2:4). In all likelihood, because the people were in rebellion to God, they would refuse to listen (Ezekiel 3:7).

Therefore it was imperative that Ezekiel knew he was being sent by the Spirit, otherwise he may have withered and withdrawn at the first sign of opposition and derision.

The Spirit did, however, assure Ezekiel that '*whether they listen or fail to listen…they will know that a prophet has been among them.*' (Ezekiel 2:5) Even though he may be rejected and ridiculed, Ezekiel would eventually be vindicated as being a legitimate prophet.

How does being 'sent by the Spirit' relate to us in our ministry?

If we know we have a message or ministry from the Lord, then we are being *sent* by the Lord.

If we know we are being sent by the Lord, then ultimately our 'mission is his mission'. 'Those who hear and accept our words on his behalf accept him, and conversely, those who reject the word of God through his servants reject the Lord himself.' (John 20:21; Matthew 10:40)[39]

Secondly, **Ezekiel must speak *God's word*.**

---

38   ibid. p. 58.
39   ibid, p. 58.

On four different occasions within this one encounter, Ezekiel was told, '*You must speak my words…*' (Ezekiel 2:7; cf. 3:1, 4, 10–11)

He was given no latitude or licence to modify or minimise the message he was to deliver. He had one responsibility—he must deliver the word of the Lord as it was given to him.

Even though his actual message was filled with '*words of lament and mourning and woe*' (Ezekiel 2:10), he was not to shy away from, nor water down, the essence of the message. This applied whether the people listened or not (Ezekiel 2:5).

How does this command apply to us? If we are rejected—even though we are lovingly and uncompromisingly preaching the Word of God—the people ultimately are not rejecting *us* but God and his Word.

For example, when Paul called the Thessalonians to live a morally and sexually pure life, he wrote that whoever '*…rejects this instruction does not reject man but God, who gives you his Holy Spirit.*' (1 Thessalonians 4:8) We must, nevertheless, keep on speaking because they are not our words, but his.

Thirdly, **Ezekiel would be safe with God's strength.**

Perhaps anticipating or neutralising Ezekiel's fear, the Lord urged him not to '*…be afraid, though briers and thorns are all around you and you live among scorpions. Do not be afraid of what they say or terrified by them…*' (Ezekiel 2:6)

Ezekiel was repeatedly told not to fear his fellow–Israelites or their words, which presumably would be words of rejection and threat. The implication being that God would keep him safe and give him strength to do what he was being called to do.

> If we uncompromisingly and fearlessly say what he's calling us to say, he will keep us safe and strengthen us.

Application

Putting these three reasons together, we note:

If we know we have a God-given ministry or message, we are being sent by the Holy Spirit.

If what we are saying is unquestionably from God and grounded in his word, we will have his words in our mouth.

If we uncompromisingly and fearlessly say what he's calling us to say, he *will* strengthen us to face every possible reaction.

For us, the conclusion of the three compelling assurances to Ezekiel is that we do not need to fear rejection!

Possible scenarios

Before concluding this chapter, let's explore three illustrative scenarios in which this example of 'do not fear' may be applied to our lives and ministries.

Sharing the Gospel

First, an obvious and important scenario is **sharing the gospel** with those who may have rejected or resisted it.

Don't be afraid to keep witnessing to someone you feel prompted to speak to even though they are outwardly resistant or have rejected the message. Keep preaching to the community to which God has sent you regardless of their hard hearts and indifference to the gospel. Maintain your gospel witness through acts of compassion despite ingratitude or people questioning your motives. Continue to live as an example of godliness and Christlike character irrespective of persecution or prejudice.

The gospel is truth. The gospel is powerful. The gospel changes lives. The gospel transforms communities. We need to be gripped by a deep-seated conviction in the gospel's inherent power.

Paul once wrote how he was compelled to preach the gospel in Rome, though it was an intimidating city—the symbol of imperial pride and power. People spoke of it with awe, but Paul spoke about it with passion. To the believers in Rome, he wrote how he was '...*not ashamed of the gospel, because it is the power of God for the salvation of everyone who believes.*' (Romans 1:16)

Prior to writing these words, he'd been imprisoned in Philippi, chased out of Thessalonica, smuggled out of Berea, laughed out of Athens, and belittled in Corinth as 'foolish'. When there may have been very good reasons to be reluctant, ashamed or embarrassed, he was not hesitant, ashamed or embarrassed. On the contrary, he was compelled to bring this life changing message to the most formidable city of his day.

What gave him such confidence? In his own words, the gospel is '...*the power of God for the salvation of everyone who believes.*'

Taking a stand on a moral or social issue

A second scenario may be **taking a stand on a moral or social issue,** even if it could mean unpopularity or alienation.

I have a friend who entered politics at a state level. The issue of legalising gay marriage was debated within his party. Despite his party's strong backing for legislation, he took a courageous stand based on his convictions to oppose the majority view.

Incredible pressure was brought to bear upon him, even from the leader, but he could not and would not change his position. His stand marginalised and stigmatised him. When his party later formed government he was sidelined from senior ministerial posts even though he had capably held senior portfolios in Opposition. Although his unwavering stand came at a cost, his conscience and character remained untarnished.

This reminds me of Shadrach, Meshach and Abednego who refused to bow the knee to Nebuchadnezzar's image because they knew that to do so would violate the second commandment to '...*not bow down to [idols] or worship them...*' (Exodus 20:5) They understood the punishment which would be given out for their courageous stand—death through incineration.

Nebuchadnezzar was infuriated by their uncompromising attitude and commanded their immediate execution. They were, however, preserved in the 'fiery furnace' by the divine presence.

Taking a stand comes at a cost, sometimes the ultimate cost of martyrdom. Nevertheless, as Bible–believing Christians we must not fear rejection in standing up for what is right and true, moral and ethical, or just and equitable—despite the ramifications.

Scripture urges us to stand strong and firm in the face of suffering for our faith (1 Peter 2:20–21; 3:14; 4:16). Specific promises are given for those who endure such persecution for Christ's sake (1 Peter 5:10; Matthew 10:39; 19:29). Buoyed by the Scriptures, the example of the apostles (Acts 5:41; 9:29; 13:50; 2 Timothy 3:12) and thousands of godly martyrs, we should be willing to pay whatever price is necessary to fearlessly stand up for what we believe.

Continuing to minister after rejection

A third scenario where Ezekiel's example may be applicable is when **we have actually experienced rejection** from a leader, congregation or community. Rejection can be a crushing experience which causes us to question our confidence, vision and call.

Whenever we feel like giving up or whenever we feel that we don't have the emotional capacity to handle any more rejection, we need to remember God's clear word to Ezekiel in connection with fear: '*You must speak my words to them, whether they listen or fail to listen…*' (Ezekiel 2:7) Put in different terms: we must not be silenced by the fear of rejection, but remain steadfast in our resolve to do what we're called to do and say what we're called to say.

The Lord promised Ezekiel his strength to discharge his prophetic calling. Similarly, by his Spirit who lives within us, the Lord provides the inward strength we need to rise above rejection and continue in our calling (Ephesians 3:16; Colossians 1:11).

Finally

From Ezekiel's example, here are some final and practical words of encouragement in the context of overcoming the debilitating poison of rejection:

- Keep speaking, even though the people you are sent to may not listen
- Keep doing what you are called to do, even though your hearers may not affirm or acknowledge your ministry
- Keep obeying, even though others fail to yield to God
- Keep believing, even though other people's words and actions may dishearten you
- Keep praying, even though some may ridicule your devotion
- Keep resolved, even though others vacillate
- Keep focussed, even though other people's words try to divert you
- Keep positive, even though many are negative
- Keep growing, even though other people have stagnated
- Keep seeing yourself as God sees you, although other people have a negative or misguided perception of you
- Keep holy, even though other people may be living questionable and carnal lives

Why shouldn't we fear rejection? Because God calls us, enables us, anoints us, envisions us, sustains us, strengthens us, indwells us, works through us and toughens us. Therefore we *can* and *must* continue in our ministry regardless of past rejection.

19

Fear that Our Best Days are in the Past

Haggai 2:3–5

We didn't have adequate equipment. It was a steep and tricky descent climbing over fallen tree trunks and sliding on loose rocks. The foliage was getting thicker as we neared the valley floor. The sun had nearly set, so it was getting increasingly difficult to see the path. We had no mobile reception and had to use the light of our phones to read the map. The creeks we had to cross were slightly swollen from recent rain. Our legs were tired. We were kilometres from where the car was parked. I asked myself, 'How did we get into this predicament?'

The day had started off well. My wife and I were on a short break with some close friends of ours in ministry at the picturesque seaside town of Lorne, located along the Great Ocean Road on Victoria's southern coast.

After a nutritious breakfast, my friend David and I decided to go on a leisurely hike through the Great Otway National Park, while the girls would enjoy coffee and a chat. We wisely went to the Tourist Information Centre to get the appropriate map before working out which route we would take. We decided on a relatively short hike of about 3–4 hours. That was the plan!

It was quite a cool day so hiking was very pleasant, except for the steep sections of the track. At the top of a ridge, we came to an intersection of tracks. Our map said that the path we were looking for was 150 metres from the juncture on the left. We walked the distance but there were no signs or tracks. Though perplexed we decided to keep looking in case the scale of the map was inaccurate.

We walked and walked but still there was no track. Studying the map again we noted there was another alternative track up further so we decided to head for that one, though the map did not specify how far it was. After hiking uphill through a great deal of mud for many kilometres, we were becoming anxious. The sun was going down and we had no idea where we were. We decided to go back the way we had come before it became too dark. It was going to be a race against time.

Back near the junction we discovered what we'd originally missed. About 10 metres (not 150 as the map indicated) from the junction there was a clearly marked track down the side of the ridge. It was now dusk, so we didn't have time to commiserate. After descending the awkward hillside, crossing the creek a number of times, and falling in once, we eventually made it out to the Great Ocean Road. From there we had another few kilometres of walking in water-logged boots back to where David's car was parked.

Our whole adventure occurred because we had inadvertently missed the sign and gone off track. A nineteenth reference to *'do not fear'* addresses people who were way off track from where God wanted them to be and what he wanted them to do. God had a great task for them, but many things had diverted their attention. So, the Lord raised up the prophet Haggai to get them back on track. Our focus passage will be Haggai 2:3–5.

Historical setting

In the last chapter, the Israelites were exiled in Babylon. Subsequently, Cyrus, king of Persia, conquered the Babylonians. In the first year of his reign, Cyrus issued an edict empowering and permitting the Jews to return to Judah and rebuild Jerusalem (Ezra 1:2–4).

According to Ezra, there were 42,360 exiles besides 7,337 servants and 200 singers who made the journey back to Jerusalem (Ezra 2:64–65).

They recognised the first order of business was to rebuild the temple in Jerusalem. Construction began almost immediately. By the seventh month of the first year after their return, they had built an altar and reinstated the prescribed sacrifices (Ezra 3:1–6).

> A general apathy anesthetises many Christians... deceptive thinking prevails.

Work on the temple proper began in the second month of the second year (Ezra 3:7–9). The first step was to lay the foundation, which seems to have been accomplished rather quickly.

When it was completed, there was an incredible and emotional celebration (Ezra 3:10–13). At this point, however, trouble began.

Trouble

Three things happened that brought the temple construction to a grinding halt.

First, some Samaritans to the north began to oppose the reconstruction and '...*set out to discourage the people of Judah and make them afraid to go on building. They hired counsellors to work against them and frustrate their plans.*' (Ezra 4:4–5)

Secondly, according to Haggai 1:2, the people, demoralised by the Samaritans' words, adopted the misguided view that it therefore couldn't be the right time to build the temple.

Thirdly, most tragic of all, the people became more concerned with their home renovations than with building the '*house of God*' (Haggai 1:3–4). Haggai's words held an incriminating accusation: '*Is this a time for yourselves to be living in your panelled houses, while this house remains a ruin?*' (Haggai 1:4)

Parallels to the contemporary church

Before we get to the crux of this chapter's point, there are some parallels from these three things to the spiritual condition of many Christians and churches today.

First, like the remnant, many believers become discouraged and demoralised by the voice of opposing people or the enemy's schemes to frustrate the work of the local church and kingdom of God. Rather than resist Satan, many just give up serving and sowing their lives into the church and kingdom.

Secondly, like the remnant's flawed conclusion that the timing was wrong to rebuild the Temple, a general apathy anesthetises many Christians. Deceptive thinking prevails: 'I'll serve *one day*, I'll get involved *one day*, I'll do what I can *one day*. It's not time, yet. I just haven't got time at the moment. It can wait!'

Thirdly, and this is again the most tragic, some are so preoccupied with their own lives, pleasure, leisure, career, bank balance or home that they totally neglect their personal spiritual growth, calling and gifting, and service in the house of God at their local church.

When God calls us into a local church, he doesn't do so with the idea he wants us to warm the pews. He plants us in a church to be part of its relational community, to serve in areas of gifting and passion, and mature in our faith as part of a growing body. We grow by engaging and serving.

Haggai's first prophecy

While the people were building their own houses, the work on the Temple ceased. During the next sixteen years no work was done at all on the Lord's house (Ezra 4:24).

The people didn't realise it, but as a result of their self-indulgence and spiritual indifference, the Lord had withdrawn his blessing (Haggai 1:5-6). The outcome was that they sank into an economic depression.

This was the scene in which God raised up the prophet Haggai. His prophetic ministry lasted just 15 weeks in the year 520 BC. Along with

Zechariah (Ezra 5:1–2; cf. 6:14), he rebuked and challenged the people to resume the construction of the new Temple.

Haggai's book contains four messages from God all marked by the date on which he received each message (Haggai 1:1, 15; 2:1, 10).

The first message called on Zerubbabel the governor, Joshua the High Priest and all the people to *complete* what they had begun (Haggai 1:7–11).

The people obeyed the voice of the Lord through Haggai and just 23 days later the work on the Temple recommenced (Haggai 1:12, 14–15).

The good old days?

However, within a few short weeks the enthusiasm of the people waned once more.

When the foundation was laid, the younger people shouted for joy, but the older people wept (Ezra 3:12–13). It seemed that the older people remembered the glory of Solomon's temple which was destroyed 66 years before. They may have thought that the new temple was deficient and inferior in comparison to the old.

In other words, the past seemed so much better than the present or future. This obviously demotivated and discouraged them from building for the future. The work seemed overwhelming, but the task seemed underwhelming.

Likewise, sometimes we, too, can live in a 'past' day, believing that the present or future could not compare to the glory of the past. We reason to ourselves, 'What's the point? It's not how it used to be. Things are done differently today. The quality doesn't seem as good or as deep. It just doesn't compare to yesterday.'

> We can become immobilised in the present and unmotivated about the future.

Consequently, we become immobilised in the present and unmotivated about the future.

Haggai's second message addressed the demotivating fear that *our best days are in the past.*

Haggai's third prophecy

Governor Zerubbabel and Joshua the High Priest (Haggai 2:2) were once again the recipients of the prophecy. The first half of the prophecy read:

> '*Who of you is left who saw this house in its former glory? How does it look to you now? Does it not seem to you like nothing? But now be strong, O Zerubbabel, be strong Joshua son of Jehozadak, the high priest. Be strong, all you people of the land and work. For I am with you. This is what I covenanted with you when you came out of Egypt. And my Spirit remains among you.* **Do not fear**.' (Haggai 2:3–5 emphasis mine)

Haggai's message initially conceded that the second Temple would not, indeed, *outwardly* compare with Solomon's (Haggai 2:3). But he would later say that what would go on *inside* the Temple would far exceed it (Haggai 2:9).

Two reasons not to fear and to get on with it

Then he prophetically urged them to be strong and get on with the rebuilding (Haggai 2:4). Based on the final words in the paragraph, '*Do not fear,*' it seems the people were despondent and demobilised because of two fears: that the future couldn't match the past and that they didn't have what it took to complete the task. The Lord gave Zerubbabel, Joshua and, by implication, the people two profound and persuasive reasons why they should resume the construction and how they could neutralise their fears.

First, the Lord promised his abiding presence while they worked ('*For I am with you*'). His abiding presence was what he had covenanted with them at Sinai (Haggai 2:5). Despite their and their forefather's sins of unfaithfulness, distrust, disloyalty, neglect and betrayal, he would continue to be their faithful God.

CHAPTER NINETEEN

In making application to Haggai 2:4, Motyer wrote: 'The key to tackling despondency is found here: stop listening to ourselves and start listening to him and his word of promise. Here the Lord spoke to them of his sufficiency: "I am with you." He offers them only his presence, for in him they have all they need (see Exodus 3:12; Isaiah 41:10; 43:2; Jeremiah 1:8; Matthew 28:20; Acts 18:9–10).'[40]

The remnant did not need to wallow in hopelessness or fear because God would be with them.

Secondly, the Lord promised through Haggai that '...*my Spirit remains among you.*' The Lord would be with the people through the presence of the Holy Spirit. In a similar vein, Zechariah prophesied to Zerubbabel that the work would be done 'not by might' (human strength or resources), 'nor by power' (human abilities or endeavours), 'but by my Spirit, says the Lord Almighty (Zechariah 4:6).'

The Old Testament is replete with references to God's Spirit abiding with the covenant people. 'The Spirit of God endows Bezalel (Exodus 31:3; 35:31), is "on" Moses, comes to "rest on" the elders (Numbers 11:17, 25–29), came on Balaam (Numbers 24:2) ...was "in" Joshua (Numbers 27:18), who was "full of" the Spirit (Deuteronomy 34:9)'[41], empowered the Judges to deliver the oppressed (Judges 3:10; 6:34; 14:6), filled the prophets with the word of the Lord (2 Chronicles 15:1) and was 'set' among the people in the Exodus (Isaiah 63:10–14) even though he was grieved by their rebellion. Now Haggai reassures the remnant that the Spirit was presently and actively remaining among them.

Likewise, the New Testament teaches that the Holy Spirit is present and active in our lives and churches. The Holy Spirit is not an impersonal force, power or experience, but a divine *Person* within the Trinity— co-equal, co–eternal and co–existent with the Father and Son (2 Corinthians 13:14).

- The Spirit is God's indwelling and empowering presence (Romans 8:9)

---
40 J. Alec Motyer, *Haggai, The Minor Prophets* (Baker Books: Grand Rapids, MI, 1998): 987.
41 ibid, p. 989.

- The Spirit brought about our new birth (John 3:5–6)
- Jesus lives within us through the person of the Holy Spirit (1 Corinthians 3:16)
- The Spirit is transforming us to become more like Jesus (2 Corinthians 3:18)
- The Spirit personalises Jesus and reminds us of his teaching (John 15:26)
- The Spirit provides empowerment to live, pray and witness (Ephesians 3:16, Romans 8:26–28; Acts 1:8)

The Spirit is active in the *life of Christians* as follows:

- The Spirit imparts (manifests) gifts into our lives (1 Corinthians 12:7–11)
- The Spirit empowers us to overcome the tempter and temptation (Luke 4:1–2)
- The Spirit enables us to crucify the old (sinful) nature (Romans 8:13b; Galatians 5:16)
- The Spirit's presence is the guarantee that we have eternal life and will be raised from the dead (Romans 8:11; 1 Corinthians 15:47–51; 1 Thessalonians 4:15–18)

The Spirit is also active in the church as follows[42]:

- The Spirit formed the Church on the day of Pentecost into the living body of Christ (Acts 2:1–4; 1 Corinthians 12:12–27; Ephesians 1:22–23)
- The Spirit formed the church to be the new and living temple of God (1 Corinthians 6:16; Ephesians 2:20–22; cf. 1 Peter 2:5; Hebrews 3:6)
- The Spirit gives gifts and graces to the members of the Church by which they can serve and minister (1 Corinthians 12:4–11, 28–31; Romans 12:6–9)
- The Spirit is the agent, under the headship of Jesus, to direct and govern the Church (Acts 13:1–3; 15:28)

---

[42] Some of these points are adapted from Conner, pp. 79–80.

- The Holy Spirit calls and equips various ministries within the Church (Acts 20:28; 1 Corinthians 12:8–11; Ephesians 4:8–12)

Do not fear

On the basis of the Lord being 'with' them and the Holy Spirit remaining 'among' them, Haggai then said, '*Do not fear*'.

These promises from God required a response: implicit faith. The people had to believe God's words through Haggai and get on with constructing the new Temple, otherwise their fear would perpetuate.

From Haggai's prophecies, what do the words '*do not fear*' mean for us?

- Do not fear abandonment – he is our faithful God despite all our failures (remember Chapter 17)
- Do not fear opposing, critical voices seeking to discourage us
- Do not fear building for the future even though the past may seem incomparably better. Keep building for the sake of the new generation
- Do not fear working as hard as we can for our local church because this is what pleases the Lord
- Do not fear making lifestyle adjustments to put God, his 'house' and Kingdom as the highest priority of our lives
- Do not fear serving with all our heart to see God's mission accomplished
- Do not fear because the Lord is always with us by the presence of the Holy Spirit

Conclusion

Let me conclude this chapter by quoting the remainder of the second prophecy. To all those who believed God's best was in the past, Haggai prophesied:

> '*"In a little while I will once more shake the heavens and the earth, the sea and the dry land. I will shake all nations, and the desired of the nations will come, and I will fill this house with glory,"* says the

Lord Almighty. "The silver is mine and the gold is mine," declares the Lord Almighty. **"The glory of this present house will be greater than the glory of the former house,"** *says the Lord Almighty. "And in this place I will grant peace," declares the Lord Almighty.'* (Haggai 2:6–9, emphasis mine)

> May we prioritise our lives and time to always put the Kingdom first.

The inadequacies of the present (Haggai 2:3) will give way to the splendour of the future. What they had experienced of God's presence in the Temple of old would be eclipsed by the future glory of the Messiah's coming. This prophetically pointed to Jesus whose redemptive ministry would make the glory of God's presence accessible and available anywhere, and at any time.

By way of application, may we prioritise our lives and time to always put the Kingdom first. May we be committed to building his 'house'. May we welcome his glory to dwell in the 'temple' of our lives (1 Corinthians 3:16; 6:19) and the 'temple' of our church (Ephesians 2:21). Do not fear that the best days of our lives and our church are in the past. Instead, let's believe for the greatest days that we and our local church have ever experienced. He is with us and indwells us by his Spirit.

20

Fear We Won't Be Able to Finish What We've Started

Nehemiah 4:13–14

It was one of those calls every pastor dreads. It was a Saturday night. Nothing can quite prepare you for it. Here's what happened. The young adult ministry of the church I was pastoring was away up on the Sunshine Coast, Queensland, for its annual retreat.

The youth Pastor, Paul, was on the line. After some quick pleasantries, I detected a subdued tone in his normally upbeat voice. 'What's happened?' I tentatively asked.

'We've had a *death* at the camp. One of the young people has died.' I was shaken but after a deep sigh, I asked, 'Who was it? How did it happen?'

It was a young man we'll call Michael. He had major health challenges. Michael was born deaf and with cerebral palsy, so he walked with a hunched back. He could sign and communicate well. His sense of humour was sharp. Everybody loved him.

No one is really sure what happened to him. He went for a long walk on a very hot day. Sometime later, some of the young people found him submerged fully clothed near the bottom of the retreat centre's pool. One of the young adults was a doctor. After retrieving Michael from the pool, the young doctor tried desperately to resuscitate him, but there was no response. An ambulance arrived within a short time, but it was too late. Michael had died.

You can just imagine the effect this accident had on the young people. A sadness and grief swept through the camp. The leaders of our pastoral team rallied as many of the other pastors as they could to drive to the camp to bring ministry, counsel and comfort to the young adults. The night service turned out to be an extraordinary time of encounter with God.

A number of days later, a funeral service was held for Michael. His mother conveyed the following story of Michael as a child.

He didn't want to go to a special school. He wanted to attend a normal state primary school, and he did. When the athletics competition was on, he wanted to compete with all the other kids (without advantages). In the distance races, the teacher wanted to give him a head start, but he refused. He wanted to start with all the other kids. He couldn't hear the starter's gun go off so he'd have to watch for the smoke from the gun. His mother said that he was, naturally, always last. Nevertheless he ran with all his heart. As he would cross the finishing line, he would throw his hands in the air like an Olympic athlete winning gold.

His attitude was inspiring. For Michael, the race was not about competing, it was about *finishing*.

Michael's inspirational example in his school races leads us to ask some searching personal questions:
- Am *I* finishing well?
- Do *I* finish what I start?
- Do *I* stay focused on what I'm called to do?
- Am *I* doing what I'm supposed to be doing or am I distracted by 'things'?

In this final chapter, we will refer to Nehemiah 4:13–14, where we find a twentieth and our final reference to '*do not fear*' in the Old Testament.

Historical background

The book of Nehemiah continues the history of the Jews returning to their own land from exile in Babylon.

Nehemiah was the king's cupbearer in the Royal Court (Nehemiah 1:11). His brother had recently returned from a trip to Jerusalem. Inquisitive about the state of the Jews and Jerusalem, Nehemiah asked about the condition of the city of his fathers (Nehemiah 1:2). His brother informed him of the deplorable state of the city's walls and gates, and the exposed feeling of the people (Nehemiah 1:3).

Upon hearing this, Nehemiah fasted, wept, mourned and prayed (Nehemiah 1:4–11). His prayers were heard. With divine favour came human favour. The king commissioned him to rebuild the walls and granted him everything that was necessary (Nehemiah 2:8–9).

Nehemiah mobilised a force and commenced the rebuilding. He faced the reality of the conditions of the wall—ruined and destroyed by fire—but this didn't concern him because he had a God-appointed task.

Opposition

Although Nehemiah and his men initially faced ridicule, sarcasm and insult, everything started efficiently and productively. They '...*rebuilt the wall till all of it reached half its height, for the people worked with all their heart.*' (Nehemiah 4:6)

But then a series of things began to happen which unsettled them. The neighbouring peoples were not only angry with the progress, but conspired to threaten and thwart the rebuilding (Nehemiah 4:7–8).

At the same time, '*the people in Judah said, "The strength of the labourers is giving out, and there is so much rubble*

> It's difficult to constantly hear negative and dispiriting information without some of it affecting us in some way.

that we cannot rebuild the wall.'" (Nehemiah 4:10) To make matters worse, their enemies started to intimidate them by saying: *'Before they know it or see us, we will be right there among them and will kill them and put an end to their work.'* (Nehemiah 4:11)

Even *'...the Jews who lived near them came and told us ten times over, "Wherever you turn, they will attack us."'* (Nehemiah 4:12)

Through the combination of all of these things, Nehemiah's men started to show the signs of discouragement. It's difficult to constantly hear negative and dispiriting information without some of it rubbing off on us or affecting us in some way.

By the way, if you are personally prone to discouragement, don't spend too much time listening to negative or disheartening people. Be careful who you listen to.

Nehemiah's response

Given the cacophony of intimidation affecting his men, Nehemiah needed to rally and focus them on the task at hand. He did two things. He called the workers together for prayer *and* he posted guards in the exposed places on the half built wall (Nehemiah 4:9, 13).

Nehemiah's responses provide us with two quick life lessons for how we can respond to people's negativity and Satan's intimidation. We, too, should pray *and* we need to be on guard in the vulnerable places of our lives, especially our thought-life.

Do not be afraid

After Nehemiah exercised decisive spiritual and strategic leadership, he spoke to his leaders and workers to remobilise them for the task. This is where we find the reference to the *'do not fear'*.

Nehemiah said, *'After I looked things over, I stood up and said to the nobles, the officials and the rest of the people, "**Do not be afraid** of them. Remember the Lord, who is great and awesome, and fight for your brothers, your sons and your daughters, your wives and your homes."'* (Nehemiah 4:14, emphasis mine)

Nehemiah gave them two keys for how they could subdue and silence the fear generated by the surrounding agitators and aggressors.

1. Remember the Lord

The first thing Nehemiah told them to do was to *'remember the Lord, who is great and awesome…'* Rather than remember the words of those threatening them, Nehemiah instructed them to remember the words and works of the *'great and awesome'* God whose work they were carrying out.

> One of the things that God continually told his people to do was to remember all the things he had said and done.

In the Old Testament, especially in Deuteronomy, one of the things that God continually told his people to do was to *remember* all the things he had said and done.[43] By doing so, the people would remember his words, works and wonders.

'Remember' is a word that requires action. It speaks of an intentional recalling and recounting to oneself all the deeds, deliverances and wonders of the Lord. To 'remember', in this context, means to recall what God has done in the past in such a way that it becomes a reality in our present circumstances. The people needed to recollect the specific things God had done for them as a way to remind themselves that what he had been in their past, he would be in their present and future.

In their people's redemptive history, they needed to remember that:
- He created the heavens and the earth by the word of his power
- He created a people for himself
- He delivered them from Egyptian captivity by displays of divine power
- He made a path through the Red Sea

---

43 For examples of the motif of 'remember' see Deuteronomy 6:12; 8:2, 18–19; 15:15; Psalm 103:2; 105:5

- He miraculously preserved and provided for his people in the wilderness
- He initiated a covenant with his people at Mt Sinai to be their God
- He revealed himself as a fearsome God whose presence would remain with them
- He judged nations which opposed and threatened them
- He fought *for* and *with* his people
- He brought them through the flooded Jordan River
- He demolished the formidable, impenetrable walls of Jericho
- He placed his Spirit upon leaders which empowered them with supernatural capacities to deliver the people
- He answered their specific collective prayers for divine intervention
- He had brought them back from exile
- He had been their faithful God despite being an unfaithful people

Likewise, whenever we find ourselves in circumstances which parallel Nehemiah and his men, we need to remember the greatness and awesomeness of God as he has revealed himself in his Word, in his Son, Jesus Christ, and in the experiences of our lives. Whenever we forget or fail to recall God's past actions, we are unknowingly making ourselves vulnerable to future discouragement and fear.

Nehemiah's antidote for the poison of their adversary's words was for the leaders and workers to remember who their God *is* ('*awesome*') and what their God had done for them as a people ('*great*').

2. Fight

After encouraging his men to remember the Lord, Nehemiah also urged them, secondly, to "…***fight*** *for your brothers, your sons and your daughters, your wives and your homes*" (Nehemiah 4:14, emphasis mine). Their prayerfulness, vigilance, positive attitude and fearlessness from remembering God would mean very little *if* they weren't prepared to fight.

Nehemiah, however, gave them a very personal reason to fight—their families and their homes. They were to fight for what was most valuable and important to them at a personal level. Others were relying on them to fight. The future of their families was dependent on them overcoming their fear and fighting through. This was a persuasive motivation.

In our battles with fear, one very important factor is our motivation. Do we have the resolve to stand strong in the heat of the battle against fear? Without the right motivation, we'll never be able to summon or sustain the necessary will power. Our motivation is the key.

For Nehemiah's men, the motivation was their families and homes—their very survival as a people.

For Michael, whose story opened the chapter, his motivation was to finish the race.

For us, our motivation should be one of absolute determination to persevere in the difficult times, on good or bad days, whether we feel strong or weak, and irrespective of favourable or adverse circumstances.

We *can* break though, we *can* overcome, we *can* prevail, and we *can* stand strong and firm against fear. To do so, however, we must make a clear definitive decision not to give in or give up until the victory is won.

Application

Nehemiah and his men faced insurmountable odds, but they refused to be cowered or crushed by fear. On the contrary, they recalled the revelation of God in their nation's history *and* they prepared to fight.

As a result, Nehemiah recorded that '...*when our enemies heard that we were aware of their plot and that God had frustrated it, we all returned to the wall, each to his own work.*' (Nehemiah 4:15) The work recommenced with the workers being ready for any sudden attack or eventuality (Nehemiah 4:16–23).

In closing this chapter on Nehemiah, there is a wonderful picture portrayed by how the men continued in their work. '...*Those who carried materials did the work with one hand and held a weapon in the other, and each of the builders wore his sword at his side as he worked.*' (Nehemiah 4:17–18)

This picture of Nehemiah's men is a great metaphor for the Christian life. Until Jesus comes we, like Nehemiah and his men, are always *building* and always *fighting*. We are fellow builders of the Kingdom of God.

In the New Testament, our work for the Gospel and Kingdom is likened to labour and work (Matthew 9:37–38; Colossians 1:29; 1 Timothy 5:17–18). And we are always in a spiritual conflict against spiritual powers until the Lord returns (Ephesians 6:11–18), therefore we need to be watchful and stand firm in our faith (1 Peter 5:8–9).

Conclusion

Given the scale of the resistance against them, it seems that some of Nehemiah's workforce feared they would never be able to finish what they had started. But through Nehemiah's strong leadership, they were encouraged to dutifully keep building with a vigilant attitude to be ready to fight at a moment's notice.

The outcome of this story was that the walls were rebuilt in 52 days (Nehemiah 6:15). When all of their enemies heard about the completion and reconstruction of the walls, they *'were afraid and lost their self-confidence, because they realised that this work had been done with the help of our God.'* (Nehemiah 6:16) What a miraculous turnaround: Nehemiah and his men were no longer afraid; their adversaries were afraid of them!

There are times when everything and everyone may seem to be against us completing what God has put in our hearts to do. Perhaps our minds have entertained the fear that we'll never be able to finish what we've started. What we have learned, however, from Nehemiah's example is that we can keep fear at bay by remaining active in labouring for the kingdom of God and by never giving in or giving up in our spiritual battles. This is how we can finish what we've started. Finish well.

Conclusion

Our journey of exploration, tracking the command *'do not fear'* through the Old Testament, began with the patriarch Abraham. His experience revealed a number of principles which lay the foundation for how we can fearproof our lives.

First we noted that the words *'do not fear'* were both a command *and* a choice. 'Fear not' was a divine directive which required a human response.

Beginning with Abraham, we saw that, whenever God issued the command *'do not fear'*, he required the person to respond proactively. This implies that overcoming fear is not exclusively God's prerogative. Human will, human choice and human response are involved. Quenching the flames of fear was a partnership between God *and* people.

As we followed this 'partnership' story by story, we discovered that the human choice to resist fear was not simply a mind–over–matter discipline, or a positive mental attitude or even the exercise of rugged will–power— even though these things are indispensable in our spiritual armoury. The narratives show that their choice not to fear was based on the revelation of God. God revealed something about his character, nature or purpose which formed the basis for *why* the person did not need to fear.

In Abraham's case, it was the revelation of God as his shield and reward (rewarder). For the children of Israel trapped between Pharaoh's forces and the Red Sea, it was the revelation of God as their deliverer. To Jehoshaphat and Judah, the revelation that their battle was the Lord's extinguished their fear and filled them with hope for the future.

Along our journey, we observed many diverse characters whose stories touch the core of our human emotions. For example, Hagar and Ishmael were rejected and banished to the wilderness and a precarious future; David was grief–stricken by the abduction of his wives and children along with the threat of his once-loyal men stoning him; and the widow of Zarephath and her son were about to eat their last meal before expecting to die of starvation and privation. In every case, however, when fear threatened to suffocate them, God met them in the depth of their pain and revealed himself as a God who would intervene for them.

Some of the people we examined faced life-threatening scenarios far worse than anything many of us will ever face. Elisha and his servant were surrounded by the formidable army of Aram; Hezekiah and the people of Jerusalem were under siege by Sennacherib and his intimidating forces; the exiled people of Judah felt forsaken and abandoned in Babylon. God did not leave his people wallowing in fear and vulnerability, but revealed himself as a God who would deliver his people.

In every chapter, we saw how each person responded to the revelation of God. Hagar picked up Ishmael and had her eyes opened to see life-hydrating water; Ezekiel prophesied despite feeling fearful; Nehemiah's men continued rebuilding the wall with their tools in one hand and a sword in the other; and Gideon overcame his insecurity to mobilise his 300 vastly outnumbered men to defeat the Midianites.

From the examples just cited, we therefore deduce a second principle: resisting fear is a thoughtful, intentional choice we make in response to the revelation of God.

This is where it gets very exciting for us as believers in Jesus as Lord and Saviour. Unlike all the characters we've studied in this book, we are not people under the Old Covenant; we are people of the New Covenant. This means that the revelation of God we respond to in our battles with fear is even fuller and greater than the people we're looked at.

The ultimate revelation of God is through his son, Jesus Christ (Hebrews 1:1–3). Through his life, suffering, death and resurrection, Jesus has conquered all the power of sin and Satan. He lives. He reigns. He is Lord. He is triumphant. He has the name above all names. His power is immeasurable. His glory is indescribable. His majesty is incomparable. He is the Victor.

Jesus now lives within us through the Person of the Holy Spirit who, as we noted, is God's indwelling and empowering presence. The Spirit's power raised Jesus from the dead, and this power now lives in us. What does this mean for us in our battles with fear? We are never alone. We do not fight this fight alone. God's Holy Spirit can empower us to overcome any and all debilitating fears so we can live a victorious life. Resurrection power is available and accessible to us in Jesus' name to defeat fear.

In addition, we have the written revelation of God in the Scriptures. God's Word is full of truth which renews our wrong and warped thinking patterns and processes (Romans 12:2; Ephesians 4:22–24). It is bursting with new covenant promises by which we can stand our ground (e.g. Romans 8:37; 2 Corinthians 3:18, 5:17; cf. Ephesians 6:11–13). Scripture resonates with the revelation of the character, nature and power of our great Trinitarian God.

God doesn't ask us to address our fears in our own strength, but to base our resistance on the revelation of who he is in his Word, what he has done through Jesus on the cross, and his unfinished work in our lives by his Spirit. As we do so, we can potentially live a life that is *fearproof*.

Appendix

Person	Fear	Revelation
Abraham	Fear that we are vulnerable to attack	God is our shield and reward / rewarder
Hagar	Fear that no one sees and no one cares	God hears our cries and will answer our prayers
Isaac	Fear that the negative cycle of circumstances will never end	God's presence will bring us through every circumstance
Jacob	Fear of the future	God's promises about the future will be fulfilled
Moses	Fear that we are trapped by our circumstances	God is our deliverer (he fights for us)
Israelites (at Sinai)	Fear of God's vengeance & disapproval	Through Jesus, we have God's acceptance and approval, and are welcome in the divine presence
Israelites (at the Jordan)	Fear of change	God has promised to be with us throughout the process of change
Joshua	Fear that we haven't got what it takes to do what God has called us to do	God has chosen us and will equip us to do what God has called us to do.
Israelites (at Ai)	Fear that our past failures will hinder future successes	God teaches us lessons from past failures that assure us of future breakthroughs
Gideon	Fear of being rejected because of how we see ourselves	God is not finished with us, but is actively transforming us

Person	Fear	Revelation
David	Fear that what God has promised will not come to pass	God will fulfil his promises
Widow of Zarephath	Fear that we will go without if we give to God	God is a God of supernatural provision
Elisha's servant	Fear of the invisible forces of darkness	God's angelic forces *for* us are infinitely more powerful than the demonic powers *against* us
Jehoshaphat and the people of Judah	Fear of defeat in a spiritual battle	The battle is the Lord's
Hezekiah and the people living in Jerusalem	Fear of being overwhelmed by what we're going through	There is a greater power with us than our adversary
Hezekiah	Fear of Satan's intimidating words	God's words neutralise the words of Satan
Exiled people of Judah	Fear that God has rejected or forsaken us	God created us to be his people, he has redeemed us and expunged our past sins
Ezekiel	Fear that our message or ministry will be rejected	God's Spirit calls us, sends us and will strengthen us
Remnant in Jerusalem	Fear that our best days are in the past	God's abiding presence through the Holy Spirit is preparing us for our future
Nehemiah's workers	Fear that we won't finish what we've started	What God has been in the past, he will be in the future…to the end

References

Boice, James Montgomery. *The Gospel of Matthew, Volume 1, The King and His Kingdom*. Grand Rapids, MI: Baker Books, 2001.

Conner, Kevin. *The Foundations of Christian Doctrine*. Blackburn, Victoria: Acacia Press, 1980.

Motyer, J. Alec. *Haggai, The Minor Prophets*, (edited by Thomas Edward McComiskey). Grand Rapids: MI: Baker Books, 1998.

Myers, Wayne. *Living Beyond the Possible*. McLean, VA: Evangeline Press, 2003.

Oswalt, John N. *The Book of Isaiah Chapters 40–66*, The New International Commentary of the Old Testament. Grand Rapids, MI: Eerdmans, 1986.

Webb, Barry. *The Message of Isaiah*, The Bible Speaks Today (Old Testament Editor, J.A. Motyer). Leicester, England: IVP, 1997.

Williams, David. *Paul's Metaphors*. Peabody, MA: Hendrickson, 1999.

Wright, Christopher J. H. *The Message of Ezekiel*, Bible Speaks Today. Leicester, UK: IVP, 2001.

About the Author

Pastor Bruce Hills (B Min, MA Theo)

Bruce has been in Christian ministry since 1984 and brings a wealth of experience and wisdom. He is known and respected around Australia for his prophetic and insightful preaching. One well-known Christian leader in Asia described him as having the 'precision of a teacher, but the fire of a prophet'. With a passion for missions, Bruce frequently travels to many nations speaking at seminars and conferences. For nine years (2000–2009) Bruce pastored one of Australia's largest Pentecostal churches. He now serves as International Leadership Development Director for World Outreach International training and equipping pastors and leaders in the majority world. Bruce has authored another book, *Praying with Power – How to Engage in a Deeper Level of Personal Prayer by Praying the Scriptures*. Bruce has been married to Fiona since 1983 and has three grown children. They live in Melbourne, Australia.

For more information on the author and to find out about World Outreach International visit www.world-outreach.com

By the same author

PRAYING WITH POWER – *How to Engage in a Deeper Level of Personal Prayer by Praying the Scriptures*

You can purchase other titles by Bruce Hills from:

www.amazon.com
www.koorong.com
www.bookdepository.co.uk
www.wesleyowen.com